Rejection **Reset.**

What Readers are Saying About
Rejection Reset

"Being involved in a project that was not going quite as well as anticipated, I allowed the nasty self-confidence gremlin into my head. "Rejection Reset" caught my eye at the right time. When I began reading the book, I realized this was not just another book on the subject, but one with substance and clear action plans to help us get through those negative times in our lives."

"The psychological mindset of being rejected, being an outsider, feeling just not belonging and isolated is quite a devastating state to survive in society. This book addresses these areas with solutions that may or may not work for every individual but at least all are worth a try to overcome this isolation."

"Being rejected can ruin anyone's day. Rejection Reset is a wonderful way to evaluate how use rejection to positively learn how to live an emotionally stronger life. With this book, there are various strategies that Scott gives his readers so that we learn how to stop self-sabotaging ourselves and reacting to our situations with more confidence."

"Rejection Reset takes you step by step through the process of overcoming your fear of rejection, and helps you understand where that fear and lack of self-esteem come from. The author explains why change is difficult and offers 5 steps to permanent change so you don't fall back into the same old habits. A very insightful book on why we act the way we do and how to change it."

"I highly recommend this book for anyone who needs a confidence boost. This book will help you gain perspective, rise above challenges, and grow as a person. I wish I had this book years ago when I got laid off from a job. Scott Allan provides a roadmap to help you gain more confidence and move past your rejection whether it was a break-up, layoff, or other situation."

"The fear of rejection can be a huge barrier preventing us from moving forward and achieving our dreams. Scott's book offers compelling arguments and actions for re-setting our fear of rejection and freeing up our personal power to build the life we want to live."

"Being rejected and dealing with the consequences of this happening to you just plain sucks. It hurts and getting over it can often be tough. That's why I really enjoyed Scott's book. He writes in a way that makes you feel like he's just talking to you, like you're sitting down having a coffee together, which is really important when trying to deal with hurt feelings."

"A Great Book for everyone to read to help you gain self-confidence! Learn how to focus on progress not perfection. You will learn from the authors own experience. There are steps, tips, action plans and exercises to help you develop the skills for facing the challenges in life so you can enjoy the life you deserve! This will help you work through your feelings of self-doubt."

"Rejection Reset is a powerful book full of actionable information. I especially liked the discussion on how we handle "the gap" - the period of time between when something triggers us in a potentially negative way and how we react - it is up to us to choose our reaction wisely. This book even goes beyond how best to deal with rejection and into how to improve our overall well-being."

"Rejection reset is more than a book on rejection. It is book about resetting your whole life and how you view yourself and others. I got so much out of this book. I love a book that challenges me to be better as a person. This book can be a game changer in your mindset if you apply the action plans."

"With laser sharp focus on core negative beliefs, and how they manifest in our lives, Scott Allan has done a stellar job of weaving his personal experiences with proven inner work techniques. What really caught my attention was the exhaustive list of messages we give ourselves, as a part of what we believe, and allows us to really examine it. The book is full or rich and real examples of how we really make ourselves small each day."

Books by Scott Allan

Check out these other bestselling books by Scott Allan. You can visit his website at www.scottallaninternational.com to stay up to date on all future book releases, or amazon.com/author/scottallan

Empower Your Thoughts: Control Worry and Anxiety, Develop a Positive Mental Attitude, and Master Your Mindset

Empower Your Fear: Leverage Your Fears To Rise Above Mediocrity and Turn Self-Doubt Into a Confident Plan of Action

Empower Your Success: Success Strategies to Maximize Performance, Take Positive Action, and Engage Your Enthusiasm for Living a Great Life

Rejection Reset: A Strategic Step-By-Step Program for Restoring Self-Confidence, Reshaping an Inferior Mindset, and Thriving In a Shame-Free Lifestyle

Rejection Free: How To Choose Yourself First and Take Charge of Your Life By Confidently Asking For What You Want

Do It Scared: Charge Forward With Confidence, Conquer Resistance, and Break Through Your Limitations

Relaunch Your Life: Break the Cycle of Self-Defeat, Destroy Negative Emotions, and Reclaim Your Personal Power

Drive Your Destiny: Create a Vision for Your Life, Build Better Habits for Wealth and Health, and Unlock Your Inner Greatness

The Discipline of Masters: Destroy Big Obstacles, Master Your Time, Capture Creative Ideas and Become the Leader You Were Born to Be

The Master of Achievement: Conquer Fear and Adversity, Maximize Big Goals, Supercharge Your Success and Develop a Purpose Driven Mindset

Undefeated: Persevere in the Face of Adversity, Master the Art of Never Giving Up, and Always Beat the Odds Stacked Against You

Fail Big, Expanded Edition: Fail Your Way to Success and Break All the Rules to Get There

Rejection **Reset**

Restore Social Confidence, **Reshape** Your Inferior Mindset, and **Thrive** in a Shame-Free Lifestyle

Scott Allan

www.scottallaninternational.com

Copyright © 2017 by **Radical Development Publications** all rights reserved.

Rejection Reset: Restore Social Confidence, Reshape Your Inferior Mindset, and Thrive in a Shame-Free Lifestyle / Scott Allan

All rights reserved. No part of this book may be reproduced in any form without permission in writing from the author. Reviewers may quote brief passages in reviews.

While all attempts have been made to verify the information provided in this publication, neither the author nor the publisher assumes any responsibility for errors, omissions, or contrary interpretation of the subject matter herein.

The views expressed in this publication are those of the author alone and should not be taken as expert instruction or commands. The reader is responsible for his or her own actions, as well as his or her own interpretation of the material found within this publication.

Adherence to all applicable laws and regulations, including international, federal, state and local governing professional licensing, business practices, advertising, and all other aspects of doing business in the US, Canada or any other jurisdiction is the sole responsibility of the reader and consumer.

Neither the author nor the publisher assumes any responsibility or liability whatsoever on behalf of the consumer or reader of this material. Any perceived slight of any individual or organization is purely unintentional.

Disclaimer

This book "*Rejection Reset*" is meant to help you on your journey to self-love, personal development and to discover the greatest human being that who has ever lived: **You**.

This book deals with a lot of sensitive issues that people struggle with, and they often need more help than a book can offer. **This book does not replace real therapy.** This book is only for informational and educational purposes and should not be considered therapy or any form of advanced treatment.

The author is not able to respond to specific questions or comments about personal situations, appropriate diagnosis or treatment, or otherwise provide any clinical opinions. If you think you need immediate assistance, call your local emergency number or the mental health crisis hotline listed in your local phone book's government pages.

The resources in this book are provided for informational purposes only, and should not be used to replace the specialized training and professional judgment of a health care or mental health care professional.

Neither the author nor the publisher can be held responsible for the use of the information provided within this book. Please always consult a trained professional before making any decision regarding treatment of yourself or others.

ISBN 978-1-9991376-4-9 (paperback)

ISBN 978-1-9991376-3-2 (hardcover)

ISBN 978-1-989599-08-2 (ebook)

Dedication

For all the brave men and women who struggle with rejection and refuse to be defeated. You are showing the rest of us that our dreams matter.

Keep pushing forward.

CONTENTS

The Pains of Rejection 3
Gearing Up for Full Engagement 11
Rejection Truths and Disengaging Critical Negativity 17
The Hypersensitive Rejectionist and Rejection Expectation 23
Making Predictable Choices 33
Shifting Negative Beliefs 39
The Cycle of Rejection 49
The Breakthrough Cycle 59
The Social Trigger Response 65
Confronting Pain Points 73
Escape Tactics and Coping Mechanisms 83
Guilt-Free Responsibility 93
Break-Free Strategies for Living Rejection Free 99
Building Social Confidence and Better Relationships 111
Twelve Habits to Reset Your Day 119
About Scott Allan 146

Free Gift

As a way of saying thanks for your purchase, I'm offering a free digital product that's exclusive to readers of the *Rejection Free Series*:

The Fearless Confidence Action Guide: 17 Action Plans for Overcoming Fear and Increasing Confidence

To learn more, <u>go to the link</u> below and gain access right now: https://www.subscribepage.com/o5i3r4

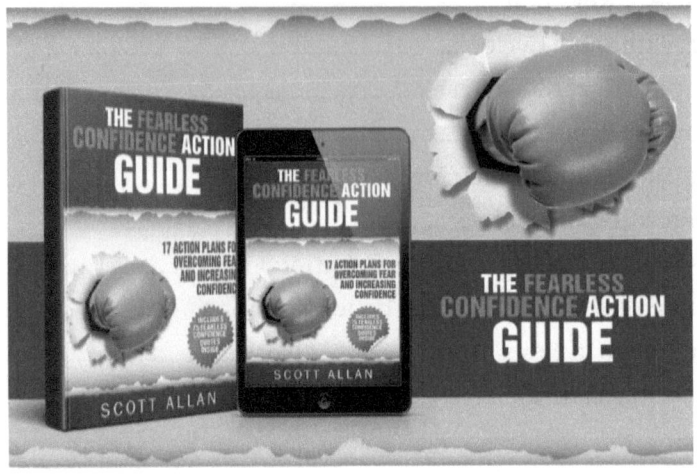

"One of life's fundamental truths states, 'Ask and you shall receive.' As kids we get used to asking for things, but somehow, we lose this ability in adulthood. We come up with all sorts of excuses and reasons to avoid any possibility of criticism or rejection."

— **Jack Canfield,** bestselling author of
The Success Principles

Introduction

The Pains of Rejection

"You have to build calluses on your brain just like how you build calluses on your hands. Callus your mind through pain and suffering."

— **David Goggins**,
American ultra-marathon runner, triathlete and author of *Can't Hurt Me*

Have you ever been in a social situation where you felt fearful and too intimidated to speak? Do you believe you have nothing to contribute to a conversation so you keep quiet most of the time? Do you feel rejected around people and feel that nobody sees the "real" you? Are you afraid to express your ideas openly because you might get a verbal put-down?

If this sounds like a familiar story, you are not alone. The fear of rejection is a dilemma that affects everyone to varying degrees: at home, at work, and in society we are continuously at war with criticism, judgment, opinions, and our desire to be accepted.

The Hurts of Rejection

According to researcher Michael Murphy at the University of British Columbia, *"Targeted rejection is central to some of life's most distressing experiences – things like getting broken up with, getting fired, and being excluded from your peer group at school,"* said Murphy, in an <u>article</u> appearing in the <u>Huffington Post</u>.

Rejection can be compared to any other illness in that, if it goes untreated, it grows worse. In fact, the rejected person can actually experience intense feelings of emotional and physical pain.

In an <u>article</u> published in the Michigan News, a recent study reveals: *"The same regions of the brain that become active in response to painful sensory experiences are activated during intense experiences of social rejection."*

Rejection can cause severe emotional pain, very similar to the pain we experience when we are physically injured. For example, being excluded from a party when everyone else you know gets invited, suddenly being dumped in a relationship, or being treated as if we don't matter. All of these can cause depression, headaches and elicit psychological fear.

The University of Michigan social psychologist, Ethan Kross states in the Proceedings of the National Academy of Sciences:

"On the surface, spilling a hot cup of coffee on yourself and thinking about how rejected you feel when you look at the picture of a person that you recently experienced an unwanted break-up with may seem to elicit very different types of pain. But this research shows that they may be even more similar than initially thought."

Psychologist and author <u>Guy Winch</u>, Ph.D., states that, "Many times rejection does 50% of the damage and we do the other 50%." What he is referring to is that when we get rejected, we begin with a stream of negative self-talk that spirals into a form of self-rejection, and, in some cases, self-hatred for oneself.

This negative self-talk could stem from any situation in which we experience rejection from a romantic relationship, a co-worker, or friend who ignores us in passing. Your emotions turn into a hypersensitive radar that starts to see rejection everywhere.

Guy Winch also states in his book, *<u>Emotional First Aid</u>*, "Rejections elicit emotional pain so sharp it affects our thinking, floods us with anger, erodes our confidence and self-esteem, and destabilizes our fundamental feeling of belonging."

Social rejection is one of the biggest self-defeating behaviors that affects millions of people both at home and at work. In their daily lives most people are not aware they are making critical choices and taking actions detrimental to their social life.

The problem is that most people who live with this affliction cling to an "emotional ledge" most of their lives. They hang on while expecting help to arrive. But it does not. Living a life of quiet desperation, the cycle of self-defeat brought about by rejection becomes seemingly impossible to break.

Many get frustrated and want a quick fix to end their pain, so they turn to addictions and bad habits to numb the negative emotions taking hold of their lives. They want to escape from feeling inferior. They want to avoid those thoughts and feelings feeding into their distilled beliefs of inadequacy. They want to be in control of their lives but they just don't know how to get to that stage.

Hypersensitivity to rejection plays a role in the success or failure of each of us. The more sensitive we are, the less empowered we feel.

Using various escape strategies, such as addiction or other negative coping mechanisms, may work in the short run. In the long term, it sets people up for failure. That rescue boat they keep hoping for never arrives and they are left alone, abandoned, and clinging for help.

There are many excuses people use to justify staying stuck in these situations. Those excuses become lies that bury the truth and keep them spinning in place. If this is you, I say it is time to do something about this. You can change the way things are. You can start right now. You can make the right choices to free yourself.

This is where *Rejection Reset* can help you.

The Purpose of *Rejection Reset*

Just like you, I know what it is like to go through life with low self-esteem and a total lack of confidence. In time, this feeds into disempowering beliefs and negative thoughts that can create heavy self-doubt. I know what it is like to struggle with personal and business relationships when your fear is the deciding factor that influences key decisions.

I know the feeling of always having to compensate for inadequacies that appear real when around certain people or social situations. It is not fun when you are always sitting on edge, waiting for someone to finally figure out the darkest secret you want to keep hidden.

Feeling like "loners" and that nobody understands us, we take to hiding behind false personas and massive egos to protect our shame-based selves. This way of life keeps us functioning below our real potential and prevents us from creating genuine relationships, especially with ourselves.

As we will see later, shame is at the core of our inferior self. We feel flawed and defective somehow. Feeling helpless to cope with these feelings because they are a part of us, and living in isolation as well as fearing that someone is going to find out our "big secret," we have built up a showcase of coping strategies to protect ourselves from harm.

My purpose and mission are to help you work through your feelings of inferiority and self-doubt. I want you to live an energized lifestyle and to develop the real skills for facing the challenges that life imposes so you can enjoy the outstanding life that you deserve.

I wrote this book not from the objective viewpoint of someone like a psychotherapist, but from the personal viewpoint of someone who has struggled with what you are experiencing.

Scott Allan: a Brief Intro

My name is Scott Allan. I am an author, rejection-free confidence coach, and personal development trainer. My books have helped thousands of people just like you to recover from the obstacles that defeat them. My mission is to provide you with the tools, life skills, and confidence to take control of your life.

I have struggled with failure and self-defeat for most of my life. Through addictions, negative behaviors, and a life of struggling to change bad habits, I have worked to overcome many obstacles on my journey toward freedom. So, just like you, I know what it is like to struggle and feel like you are spinning your wheels. I know what it is like to feel completely alone on the journey.

I know that change is not easy. If you have nobody giving you advice or guiding you along the way, it is easier to give in to the lesser path. I do not want you to give up; you deserve the best in life, and if you work on yourself just a little bit every day, you can experience the full benefits of what I am going to teach you. So do not wait. The time to take action is today.

Even if you have a strong desire to break your limitations, this will not happen until you disengage the core negativities that are keeping you stuck. Thanks to the techniques I am going to share with you in this book, you can begin to live the life that you have always dreamt of but could never quite reach.

You see, if we are not in charge of our lives, someone or something else is. If we are not making choices that empower us, we are making choices that limit us.

If you are grappling with negative emotions and thoughts that keep you stuck, and you want to break free, then you are in the right place. I cannot claim to have all the answers. But, I can tell you that the ideas and strategies in this book come from my own personal experiences, and what I found that helped me get through a lot of the past stuff that was controlling my life. I have made a lot of progress because of the wisdom and teachings past mentors shared with me. I want to share this wisdom with you now.

Why *Rejection Reset* is a Good Fit for You

Rejection Reset is for anyone looking to overcome the hurdles and challenges of dealing with social rejection. The rejection "pain" can take place within your mind [self-rejection] and out there in the real world.

This is a program full of easy-to-implement steps that you can begin to put into action right away and see real results. You will learn how to identify the triggers and behaviors that perpetuate the cycle of defeat, learn why you feel inferior to everyone else, and develop the confidence to take action so you can start to live a more fulfilling lifestyle.

You will learn how to:

- Take immediate action against the fear of rejection so that you can feel great about yourself again

- Conquer your painful points of jealousy, inferiority, inadequacy and vulnerability

- Stop trying to measure up to other people and just be who you are

- Break the mindset of the rejectionist and replace it with healthy, positive habits that focus on creating the life you have always wanted

- Disengage the faulty negative beliefs that kill your motivation and productivity

- Implement powerful strategies that work to replace the worn-out techniques that only serve to defeat you

- Build healthy social relationships with people and get confident with yourself in social settings

- Implement the 6-step process for creating lasting change and breaking the negative cycle

- Practice twelve daily habits and build a new routine to keep you from slipping back into a lifeless rut

Later on, we will look at the coping strategies people use to survive through life when they don't know any other way. I can show you how to create new methods so that you are no longer running away but are taking a stand that empowers the real you. You do not have to just survive anymore; you can learn to live and be yourself.

In this book, I will talk about the cycle of rejection and how it manifests itself through daily repetition of bad habits. I have written this material to be short and concise. There will be no long psychobabble explanations or psychotherapy exercises to probe into the last twenty years of your life and relive painful issues of the past. By the time you have finished reading this book, you will have displaced the rejectionist mindset.

If you are all in, keep reading. In chapter 1, you'll learn seven actions you can take right away to start moving towards a rejection free state of mind.

"As humans, we're reading books every day to try to figure out how to be someone else. What we don't do is go inside, turn ourselves inside out, and read our own story. You have to look inside to find out what you really want."

— **David Goggins**

Chapter 1

Gearing Up for Full Engagement

"Most fears of rejection rest on the desire for approval from other people. Don't base your self-esteem on their opinions."

— **Harvey Mackay**

It is recommended that you put yourself into a clear frame of mind before reading. Induce a relaxed state by focusing on your thoughts and breathing. If you have any negative thoughts that creep into your mind during the next chapter, try to push them away and focus on your positive attributes. We are here to learn and to heal.

Six Strategies You Can Practice Today

As we begin, I want to give you six strategies to put into practice as you read through this book.

1. Be Good to Yourself

One of the biggest hang-ups that defeat many people is the habit of beating up on themselves. They continuously repeat negative thoughts to themselves like "I am not worthy of love," "I am no good," or "I have nothing of value to give to anyone."

They do this through reinforcing conditional behaviors that defeat their actions. By beating themselves up through negative self-talk and harsh criticism, they minimize their personal value by buying into the "I'm worthless" mindset.

This is the great lie that perpetuates itself and grows stronger over the years. The more we repeat these negative messages to ourselves, the more real they become. This has to end if we are to expand beyond our current state.

What I want you to do is give yourself a break here. You are not perfect, but by reading this book you have taken a positive step by making a clear decision to improve yourself.

You could be hard on yourself because somebody else was hard on you. It is time to step up and start being good to yourself. Later on, I will show you the strategies for dealing with nasty negatives. You'll learn how to turn words of self-defeat and limited thoughts into empowering positives that create long-term growth and change.

2. Observe Your Reactions

Starting today, observe how you react to challenging situations. How do you feel around people you think are better than you? What thoughts are going through your mind that devalues your self-worth? When do you feel irritated? Angry? Fearful? Rejected?

This observation is an important step. For now, you don't have to figure anything out. Just watch how you react. You will start to see a pattern develop that you have not noticed before.

Reactions are conditioned behaviors that take the place of common sense and wisdom. By starting to notice your reactions now, you can develop better ways to handle situations that used to baffle you.

Overreacting, or reacting out of fear, is a coping strategy when we feel powerless to deal with difficult situations. We will get into some techniques in the following chapters on how to handle our reactive state so that we can develop a proactive position instead of just letting everything get to us.

3. Focus on Progress, Not Perfection

Perfectionism is a good thing sometimes. It can push us toward greatness instead of settling for mediocrity. It can also be an obstacle that gets in the way of making steady progress in our lives. Afraid of making mistakes, we try to do everything perfectly the first time to avoid failing. In the end we end up stalling and put off taking any kind of action.

We have a strong tendency to do things perfectly or not at all. When reading through this material, put aside the perfectionist and focus on progress that moves you ahead one step at a time. Five things done well are better than one thing done perfectly (and it is never perfect anyway).

Perfectionism is a lie that keeps you stuck. So step back and take it easy. Give yourself space to grow. Allow yourself to make mistakes. I am not perfect; you are not perfect. But you can be perfectly okay.

4. Keep an Open Mind

In this book, I ask that you have an open mind to the ideas and thoughts I am going to share with you. You do not have to accept everything, and not everything may apply to you. But when you are working through this and something suddenly clicks or stops you in your tracks, it could be a sign that something needs more attention.

Focus on the areas of your life that need adjustments. Work to replace what you have to so that you can move forward with your life. Keep in mind that you can create the lifestyle you want. You are not inadequate or flawed, as you may have been led to believe. Keep reminding yourself that you are an exceptional human being and you deserve the best.

Get into the habit of talking to yourself every morning before you leave the house. Practice having this silent conversation with yourself several times a day for relaxation. Focus on calming the voices inside your head that ramble on without meaning. By keeping an open mind, you will feel more relaxed and focused, and this will help you to deal with everyday situations that you find difficult.

5. Give Yourself Time to Heal

I do not want you to get overwhelmed with the process. Personal growth is a work in progress. Your success takes a series of small steps over a period of time. It is not the size of the jump you make that counts, but the number of steps you take along the way. There is no rush. Steady persistence is the key.

This is important, because if you are anything like I was, you will end up quitting soon, as I did many times in the past. I started something, expecting to have amazing results in a week. But when I was not completely transformed I gave up. I started to look for the next quick solution. This led back to my old self-defeating behaviors that worked in the short term because they were reliable.

Just remember, there are no quick fixes. But, by taking action just a little bit every day, you will build up a powerful reservoir of confidence, self-esteem, and discipline. Take things slowly and give yourself room to explore.

6. Visualize Your New Outcome.

Start to think about what you want to do with your life. Imagine yourself overcoming rejection and feelings of inferiority. See yourself doing, being, and having what you once only dreamt about. You can start to do this right now. Get focused and look at where you are today.

If you are in a bad place emotionally, then that is where you are. It is okay. Everyone has to start from somewhere. We do not have to wait for a perfect moment or the right circumstances to begin; just start from where you are at. The journey ahead of you is unfolding, as it needs to.

Lao Tzu said, "A journey of 1,000 miles begins with a single step." I want you to think of every day from now on as the next step and focus on the goal you are moving toward.

Do not look back and wish that things had been different. They will never be different. You can start to look at the situation differently. Think of every day as a new beginning full of opportunities. What happened yesterday or ten years ago is in the past. This does not mean you should just pretend nothing happened, but know that you are not the only one with a past that was not perfect. What you do today is what matters.

Visualize the life that you have always wanted to have, and not the one you feel stuck with. Visualize yourself doing, being, and living the best possible way you can. Start to think deeply about the direction in which you are now heading. Imagine where you could be in two years, five years, and ten years down the road by committing to a plan of action. The reality you can imagine is the life you can have, if you really want it.

You can choose your own way right now. You can stand up and say no more. You can set your own standards for living instead of the self-imposed limitations that were thrown onto you.

Do not put your life on hold anymore; it is time to make a serious shift in the way you think, feel, and take action.

Chapter Recap

In this chapter, I gave you six actions you can take:

1. **Stop beating yourself up**: Be aware of the reinforcing conditional behaviors that defeat your positive actions. Don't buy into the idea that you are worthless because you are afraid. Everyone is afraid. It is how we deal with it that matters.

2. **Observe your reactions**: How do you react to challenging situations? Do you try to avoid them or run away? By starting to notice your reactions now, you can develop better ways to handle tough situations.

3. **Focus on progress, not perfection**: We are not here to be perfect. We just want to make improvements in how we live our lives and live without hiding. Don't let your fears fail you.

4. **Keep an open mind**: Focus on the areas of your life that need adjustments and work to replace what you have to so that you can move forward with your life.

5. **Give yourself time to heal**: There are no quick fixes. By taking action just a little bit every day, you will build up a powerful reservoir of confidence, self-esteem, and discipline.

6. **Visualize your new outcome**: See yourself where you want to be in one, five, or twenty years from now. Use that mental image as a goal to strive for.

We have a lot to cover so let's not waste any time.

Are you ready?

Turn to the next page and let's begin.

Chapter 2

Rejection Truths and Disengaging Critical Negativity

"Shame is the most powerful, master emotion. It's the fear that we're not good enough."

— **Brene Brown,** author of
The Gift of Imperfection

Do you remember the last time that you were rejected by someone? Was it a romantic rejection? Were you rejected in a social group? Did the bank refuse your loan? A group of friends had a night out and you're the only one who didn't get an invitation—and you found out after they posted a group photo to Facebook?

Regardless of how it happened, I think we can agree that rejection is a painful experience. It can cause depression, anxiety, and, in many cases, mental health issues as well as physical symptoms.

According to a study in the Journal Proceedings of the National Academy of Sciences, the experience of rejection can do intense physical harm to the extent that our brain releases opioids to combat this pain.

But how do we stop from getting rejected? How do we reduce the chances of rejection? How do we avoid rejection?

These are legitimate questions people have asked me over the years. I will answer these questions in the rest of the book and give you solid strategies to implement as you deal with rejection in a more proactive and logical approach.

The Path of the Rejectionist

Here are five truths about rejection that we will get out into the open right now, before we get on with the rest of the book. Understanding these simple truths will help you to be realistic about rejection and give you greater perspective in dealing with it.

Truth #1: You will experience rejection many times throughout your life.

If you have never been rejected, you have never really tried anything challenging or risky. Rejection belongs to those people who tried and were turned down. By avoiding rejection, we place ourselves in a worse situation: the circumstances of never getting what we truly want.

You may be clever in dodging the perils of rejection, but you'll end up on the rocks just the same. This book is a guide to teach you, not how to avoid rejection, but, on the contrary, how to handle it when it does happen. Notice I said "when" and not "if." You have to accept rejection as a part of everyday life. It is also a critical formula for success.

Truth #2: The solution is internal, not external.

It is easy to think rejection is all about other people pushing us away. But actually, your reaction to rejection is most of the battle. It is how we view ourselves when we are rejected that sets the stage for what comes next.

Was I rejected because of something I did, a flaw that I have, or some hidden character defect that everyone but me can see? One of the core truths is that our internal thoughts and beliefs are deciding factors when we interpret a rejection experience.

Was I turned down because I am no good, or the other person just has no need for what I am offering right now? When we analyze our own internal feelings and thoughts, we can uncover the critical beast that lives there. It is the child that was harshly criticized, the young adult that shied away for lack of confidence around people, or the shame of expressing oneself.

Truth #3: People will judge, but they are not a jury.

People say things all the time. They complain about each other, they express dissatisfaction, and ultimately, when they cannot resolve a situation to their benefit, they will judge and condemn the other by pointing the finger.

As a rejectionist, we take this very personally. What if someone doesn't like me? What do I do? How can I gain their acceptance? How can I set this straight?

Before you try to patch up a big hole, analyze the situation for a moment. The people who judge: are they perfect? Have they been blessed with anything that you haven't?

When you take the time to think with an open mind about the opinions of other people, you may realize that they are judging the world based on:

1. a belief system.

2. a point of view that is not 100 percent accurate.

3. a fear-based mind.

We tend to be hurt by the opinions and judgments of others. Their words and actions, directed against us in a negative way, switch on our rejection sensitivity. This creates stress, fear, and anger. But the truth is, most of the time the opinions of people are based on inaccurate facts.

A point of view is just that—an imperfect opinion. Remember this: most people react out of fear, which leads them to faulty conclusions. Don't build your emotions on illogical claims.

Truth #4: You have nothing to lose.

We try to protect what we are afraid of letting go. We cover what we don't want to lose. Is it any wonder why we are so fearful? Can you imagine what you would gain if you let go of the fear of loss? My guess is, you would get everything you've ever wanted—and then some. But we try to protect ourselves too much. We put up defenses and ready the walls against certain attack. If they want what you have, they'll have to scale your emotions to get it.

There is nothing to lose if you have nothing to lose. When you spend all of your efforts to protect yourself against being injured, you are reinforcing the fears of rejection that are making you fearful.

Allowing yourself a certain level of vulnerability is a good thing. People who recover from rejection recognize that allowing people to see them as they are, while it does increase your chances of being emotionally injured, is the best way to start growing internally. Later on we will look at the ways vulnerability can open up doors for you instead of keeping them closed.

Truth #5: Your past is not your future.

If a child is raised in a family that is emotionally absent, critical, or dysfunctional, these will undoubtedly be passed down to the child. Your shame-based self and the fear of rejection started early. It did for me, too. But it doesn't have to continue.

Your past is not the future unless you decide that it is. In this case, you will continue to play out the same failed reactions, habits, and behaviors you have learned early in life. We can stop this behavior from today.

Over the years, we create coping mechanisms and escape strategies (more on this later) and we make our way into the world full of fear, doubt, low confidence and low self-esteem. The injured child is what we left behind. It is a child who wanted unconditional love and acceptance but never got it. However, we can give this to ourselves; we can be good parents to our inner child.

This recovery is a process, and there are no quick-fix solutions. But you can have success and begin to build your life, creating a new mindset and set of beliefs that work to dig you out of a rut and put you on the right track to having greater confidence and life-fulfilling experiences.

Your Response to Rejection

When something happens to trigger your feelings of rejection, we go through a series of painful emotions. The first instinct is to avoid or flee from the person or situation that is causing this distress. To defend ourselves against the situations and people who could reject us, we chose to avoid rejection at all costs. We became negative and pessimistic toward any kind of rejection. This negativity morphs into a hypersensitive condition where we start to see rejection everywhere.

The rejection factor, as time progresses, molds itself into a self-fulfilling prophecy. Your core beliefs, accepted long ago by the subconscious as being real, act as the blueprints for all future experiences. In the case of someone who suffers from rejectionism and the need for approval, every action you take, every decision made, is in alignment with your emotions, beliefs, and thoughts.

If this were based on the core strategies of your rejectionism, you would be choosing a path that leads to bad results. For example, this can be something that makes you inadvertently sabotage your efforts, or an addiction that you cannot give up because the rewards are too tempting.

The result is that you create a life built on a weak foundation. Over time the fear manifests itself into a full-blown phobia. This tremendous fear leads to further isolation, poor choices, and emotional dysfunction on many levels. You may have created a system by which you sabotage your success in work or relationships because you know, deep down that it isn't going to work out anyway.

Your life, and the future ahead of you, plays out as a self-fulfilling prophecy. Your thoughts lead to actions that build on choices based on the fear of rejection. The thoughts you develop will manifest into reality. When negative emotions take over and, you run your life from the foundations of a negative base, you can only expect more of the same.

When you are raised as a child to think less of yourself, to believe in your fears, and to stay out of sight and out of mind, those characteristics grow to define you as an adult. You will then operate from a place of unworthiness. Driven by your negative beliefs that you are not worth very much and that everyone is better than you, a flawed reality merges into your existence.

This feeling of unworthiness is the great lie that we are going to expose and dissolve. You have been living a lie. It is an illusion of the worst kind where you believe that at the very core, you are born different. You are different, and so, you learn to stay out of sight. In other words, you act as if you do not exist.

We can change that here. In the following chapters of this book I have outlined a program for you to put into action. By the time you are finished you will be able to deal with rejection, handle anything that comes your way, and push forward no matter what fears you are grappling with.

Chapter Recap

Using rejection truths to disengage critical negativity all starts with you. The fear of rejection, the need to be accepted, and the lengths that we will go to achieve this acceptance are remarkable.

Remember: there are things you can control in life. And there are many things you cannot. We have to distinguish what it is you have power over.

Is it other people's emotions, attitudes, opinions, and moods? No. We have no control over any of this. Yet, we allow ourselves to be governed by the attitudes and approval of others. This erroneous governance is how we become sensitive to rejection. By allowing ourselves to reject who we are, it makes it easier for others to reject us as well.

Imagine how your life would change if you learned to control your response to fear, rejection, and criticism? Can you visualize the switch in direction your thoughts would take? The increase in contacts and relationships you could build? How little stress you would have and the ability to let negativity just roll away from you, because you know that you are the creator of your own internal voice?

You would be able to change everything and anything at will.

In the next chapter I will introduce you to the hypersensitive rejectionist and what it means to live with "rejection expectation." You will learn to become a better social conversationalist and communicator—not just with other people, but also with yourself.

Chapter 3

The Hypersensitive Rejectionist and Rejection Expectation

"Nobody can make you feel inferior without your consent."

— **Eleanor Roosevelt**

One of the defining characteristics of someone who struggles with rejection hypersensitivity is that you come to expect rejection as an automatic response to nearly every situation. It is a combination of low self-esteem, confidence, and a host of negative beliefs that point to one thing: I am not worthy. I am inferior to everyone around me.

When you meet someone for the first time you put on an air of confidence that serves to protect you during the interaction. One reason most rejectionists fail at developing strong, long-term relationships is because most interactions are designed on purpose by the rejectionist to be short term.

You avoid any deep or involving relationships if it can be helped. Why do we do this? It takes a lot of energy to appear confident and fearless. Inside you do not feel normal, and your subconscious has been programmed to tell the truth. The reasoning behind this strategy is to, "get out while you can" before they find out just how dull and boring you really are.

Dealing with Rejection Expectation

Rejection expectation is an emotionally painful situation. It keeps you isolated, because the pain of being rejected is so great that it is better to be alone where nobody can get to you. When you expect people to not like you because you just don't fit in, this expectation becomes a self-fulfilling prophecy.

You are awkward and uncomfortable around others. You keep conversations short and time spent with one person at a minimum. During conversations you may suddenly go quiet and appear to the other person as disinterested and detached. They start looking for somebody else to converse with, leaving you "at the table" so to speak.

When you see that same person laughing and having a good time with others because they could not be with you, it reinforces the false truth that you already believe to be true: You are unworthy and incapable of forming new relationships.

Bonding with people is an uphill battle for people dealing with rejection issues. We are always on guard, fighting our inner demons for dominance over a fragile mind. It is a vicious cycle of perpetual self-rejection. Other people have nothing to do with it. We might tag them as the problem, but in fact, you are at war with your own beliefs and insecurities.

Everything you are feeling, all those negative emotions that create anxiety and panic when socializing, are self-made fears that you have created. Somebody else may have planted the seed ages ago, such as a critical parent or guardian, but throughout the years the seed has been taken care of by the master gardener: **You**.

When we can accept responsibility and own our feelings, everything changes. You gain a greater sense of self-control. You raise your confidence level right away. You become a better communicator because you remove your thoughts from concern over what other people are thinking. It is this obsession with, "what will they think?" that perpetuates the rejection cycle.

Socializing and meeting new people is just one form of rejection expectation. Rejection expectation takes place in:

- Job interviews ["I know they won't hire me because I don't have what it takes."]

- Romantic relationships [She'll dump me as soon as she finds someone better."]

- Social situations/Out in public ["You see, they just ignored me and walked right by."]

- Applying for a loan at the bank ["What's the point in applying? They always turn me down, anyway."]

- College applications ["They won't take me. My grades aren't good enough to get in. Besides, I was never good at studying in school].

- Asking for something ["Why bother asking, he will just say, 'NO,' again. People are always refusing my requests."]

This fear is so deep that rejectionists will even avoid filling out an application form for fear of being turned down. When you hear NO, it fulfills the expectations that what you feared was true all along: "I'm not good enough to have this thing." This compounds the embedded belief that *'I will always be at the lower rung of the ladder, picking up the scraps that nobody else wanted.'*

When you live this way, change becomes an impossibility. It can form into a stagnant routine that, although you may not be completely comfortable with it, will keep you stuck in the same place [an unhealthy relationship, a bad workplace] because the reality of going through the rejection phase repeatedly is too painful. It becomes a lose-lose situation: "Damned if you do and damned if you don't!"

Talking Down to Yourself: The "Voices" of Damnation

As we will see later on, your subconscious mind has been programmed from an early age to believe, develop habits, and talk to you in ways that either support you or destroy you. These messages come at you from deep down under. These are buried under years of conditioning and life experiences that molded the person you are today.

Take a moment to sit relaxed and comfortably. Just let yourself go and relax your mind. Let go of your thoughts. Do not force your thinking in any other way; let whatever thoughts you have flow through you without trying to change them. Then just let them go.

By observing firsthand the thought patterns you create—consciously or unconsciously—you can see the patterns of rejection and the process your emotions and correlated thought patterns play out in times of crisis.

In my own personal observations, what I noticed after stepping out of myself is that, when confronted with a situation that I can feel rejection creeping in, there is an internal dialogue that starts up. Those feelings of isolation, loneliness, and that urge to flee, are underlying beliefs that what is happening is real and it is all my fault.

There is an internal dialogue that starts up: "You are the reason people will not like you. There is something wrong with you that separates you from everyone else."

It is this same feeling every time that takes place no matter where you are, and because it is so repetitive, it must be true. Years of conditioning have not been kind.

In the end, there can only be one conclusion:

Nobody rejects you any harsher than you reject yourself.

For most of us, the rejection phase begins long before you enter the room, meet someone new, or give that awe-inspiring speech you have spent weeks preparing for. While it is true some people do not care for you and may even think you are boring, this does not make it universally so.

If someone doesn't like you, it might hurt a little; but if you have those same feelings toward yourself, this can turn into real suffering. We have to relearn how to be kind to ourselves, and to shut down those voices that insult, criticize and condemn. That is not who you are but the voices of a mind still attached to past events. We have a strong tendency to repeat painful experiences that occurred, even decades past, because we haven't truly let them go.

The imagination of a rejected person is a powerful force. While it keeps the victim separated and alone for protection, the imagination lives out its true desires: To be one with the crowd, to go anywhere and be anyone, to be known and famous and loved. But reality eventually comes crashing back in.

We know that we want so much but because fear runs deep, we hold ourselves back from asking for anything. We are forever on the outside wanting it all but too scared to take that leap forward.

If you are reading this book and have made it this far, it is because you can relate to at least a few of the situations here. Now, we need to take action to change, and it has to be a set of proven principles applied repetitively to bring you from that stage of nothingness to one of greatness.

You could be a different person on the inside by next week. You could be acting differently, talking differently, and even working in a different profession. That is, if you desire to take the steps to get you there. If you stay committed and dedicate a part of your day toward recovering, you will start to gradually feel good. Then, good will become great and in time, you will become extraordinary.

Going on the Defensive

Overly sensitive people tend to get defensive when they feel attacked or criticized. In many cases what is mistaken as an attack on character could simply be prodding fun, or someone making an innocent joke. In other situations, it could be an evaluation at work or, you are being blamed for something that isn't your fault.

Whatever the case, the reaction is to take a stand and counterattack the blame. But this can do more damage than good. People who fight back tend to lash out at times without provocation. You might think that you just had to do it when, in fact, the other person meant no real harm.

The other example is when you are being ostracized or criticized; it could be that a co-worker or your boss has just gone off the deep end and you happened to be in the way. Often a counterattack may be more aggressive than the actual attack in the first place. After, you might feel ashamed or embarrassed that you had reacted so strongly, and once you do, you cannot take it back.

Taking a defensive stance puts you on edge. You are constantly ready to fight back and win the argument. I have done this and felt pretty horrible after realizing that the other person wasn't acting aggressively or trying to be critical. It was all in my own head, and I had built it up that he or she had it coming anyway. In the end I only ended up hurting myself.

There is a lot to say for exercising cautious self-control. I know it is not easy but, being defensive acts like a built-in mechanism. You learned to act this way from childhood in response to pain or being rejected.

Now, in adulthood, you revolt against any kind of critical comment, even when it is constructive. Even worse is that it drives people away from you and makes them overly cautious when approaching you about something.

People with hypersensitivity struggle in work-related environments that involve teamwork or communicating with people of authority. It is always "the other guy who did it" and so, unable to see beyond blaming everyone else around them, they reject any proposal for improvement.

Here are three action steps to push you beyond hypersensitivity and develop a resilient mindset. You will become less sensitive and more active in your approach towards others. Focus on one strategy at a time. Move into the next tactic when you are feeling ready.

1. Identify your assumptions. More often than not we are guessing what people think about us. Most of our assumptions are based on fears that stem from past experiences. If we were rejected in the past, people will continue to throw rejection after rejection at us. It becomes an endless loop of personal negativity we throw at ourselves. But it goes without saying that, what you expect from the world is what you will get.

We attract the things that we assume are true. If you walk into a room and you 'assume' that people are going to ignore you or leave you out of the conversation that is what you will see in very interaction. You will actually look for it and when you find it, you will be able to confirm your assumptions as coming true.

So let's come back to reality. Take a moment to observe the assumptions you have about yourself and the world around you. Ask yourself, "Is this assumption I have true, or is it just my own fear talking? Do people really think this about me?"

When we identify the assumptions that we have, it puts things in perspective. In most cases, hypersensitivity is all about how we think the world perceives us. The cure to this is not to focus on how others view you but on how you view yourself. Do you feel confident? Are your thoughts in alignment with the person you want to be? Are you tearing yourself down, or expecting someone else to do it?

Once you have tagged your false assumptions, you can work on dismissing them. We have a strong tendency to reject ourselves before anyone else can. This is like giving the world permission to do so. The moment you stop rejecting yourself, the world will no longer matter.

What other people think, judge or assume about you will not matter, because your confidence is not built on the opinions of others. It can only come from within you. Remember what I discussed earlier: we are not basing our recovery from rejection on the opinions of the world but how we think and feel about ourselves.

2. Don't accept everything someone says as the truth. People are right sometimes…and wrong more times than they are right. Just because someone doesn't agree with you doesn't make him or her right. Also, just because everyone agrees with you doesn't mean that you have no flaws. Not all criticism is valid, so this is why we need to step back and evaluate what is being said.

People can be wrong in their opinions but we can find a good message in the harshest of critics at times. Open your mind up to the possibilities and stay fixed on seeing the truth. If you are not sure if what is being said is the truth, try asking someone. A close friend or colleague will often be more honest if you ask them.

3. Take it now, work it out later. One of the pitfalls of dealing with our sensitivity is that we are always on edge. We are ready to defend ourselves at any moment. When a critic jumps in and says something derogatory or critiques our performance at work, we are ready with teeth bared. But what if there is some truth to what they say? What if what we perceive as criticism is really an effort to help us out?

If you are sensitive to criticism, as many people are, you have your ego on alert and your pride is ready to take action. But remember that anything you say in the heat of the moment will be remembered.

Suggested action: take the remarks or criticism people give you and take time to reflect on what has been said. If someone made a comment about your report, read the paper over again to look for areas of improvement. There are people who will complain about you and are unhappy with an action you took, work you did, or the way you handled a certain situation.

The rule of thumb is, take it now but work through it later. Take time to reflect on their feedback. Look for ways you could use that feedback to improve your relationship with others and make better improvements in your own life.

Chapter Recap

It takes great patience to be kind to yourself. If you are sensitive to rejection, it hurts. Consider that the emotional pain isn't necessarily coming from the other person but from within yourself. We beat up on ourselves when we don't get it right, or when we think we fail to please someone else. To get beyond our over-sensitivity requires us to be diligent with our actions.

This attention to our own reactions means when you come across a critical person, remember that they might have a lesson to teach us. If not, you can decide to listen to what was said or brush it aside.

Don't mistake good criticism for complaining. A complainer has nothing to add. They have one goal and that is to tear down another so they can feel justified in their arguments. You can sweep this aside. If someone complains about you when you aren't around and you catch wind of it, confront that person. They may deny they said anything but at least you know there isn't any validation to anything they say.

In the next chapter we will get into **predictable choices** and what it means to make choices based on the fear we are experiencing in the moment.

Chapter 4

Making Predictable Choices

"It is impossible for you to be angry and laugh at the same time. Anger and laughter are mutually exclusive and you have the power to choose either."

— **Wayne Dyer**, bestselling author of
The Power of Intention

Rejection is a painful experience when we don't have the tools or strategies to deal with it effectively. Without proper support or guidance, you can spend your life fending off critics and staying below the rejection radar so as to avoid dealing with the pain of being told NO, or just ignored altogether.

When you are living in a place of constant fear such as the fear of being rejected or the fear of meeting people, it directly affects the quality of the choices you make.

Here is an example: Let's say you wanted to work in a new field that would be more in line with your goals, but that industry requires you to engage with people and get very personal. An example of this would be a sales position. You might avoid that kind of job, even if you really want it, because of the social pressure you feel of putting yourself out there where dealing with rejection is a part of the job.

Likewise, having a fear of job interviews you decide to stay in the same line of work, not because you want to, but because you need to avoid getting rejected in an interview. For years I stayed stuck in a job because of this. I had anxiety when I even typed up my resume. The jobs I wanted had certain requirements that I didn't have so I avoided them. Excuses like: "Oh, I'm sure they have already found somebody else," or, "I am too old to work there now anyway." The excuse was my escape tactic to keep me away from actually taking action.

Choosing the Predictable Pathway

When you operate from that place of fear, you choose the predictable pathway. Predictable situations, even if they are painful, are comfortable and we feel that we are in more control of the outcome.

By trying to control fear, we end up creating a level of anxiety that keeps us stuck in emotional pain. By escaping into our place of comfort, what we think of as a safety net is really a cage. You will never grow or expand beyond your fear when you choose to stay scared.

Here is another example. A girl named Sally wants to approach Jeff to ask him out. But Jeff intimidates her because he is popular, well educated, and seems very confident of himself. Sally hesitates and, even though she has had several chances to approach him, she has anxiety and fears that he will say "NO."

She starts to make excuses:

- *"I'm too busy for dating anyways."*
- *"I'm sure he has a girlfriend or he is probably married."*
- *"I'll approach him when I've lost more weight."*
- *"I'll wait until he notices me first."*

The excuses validate the behavior and sway our choices. You can then take the predictable path without feeling any shame or fear of the other person saying no. Sally will then find someone that is either at the same level as her or beneath her somehow. She is never fulfilled in the relationships she settles for, but she can feel comfortable in the situation knowing there is less risk in rejection.

These situations have a common theme. Both people made choices that keep them stuck at the same level. They never do anything to better themselves or go after the job, the relationship, or the life that they really want.

If your choices are based out of fear of looking silly, failing, or being turned down, you choose the predictable path that is safe. You can't lose. There is no risk involved. You might think you are winning out, but let's face it, you will never get what you want. You will spend the rest of your days envious of the people who have what they want, and wishing you could be more like that.

In the end, people settle for what they can get or whoever will have them, instead of going for what they could have if they just pushed past the pain threshold of vulnerability.

The same can be said for the work we do. Did you know that over half the people employed are unhappy in their work? If so many people don't want to be at the place they are working, why do they stay? Many people stay stuck because of the belief that they won't get anything better. Others would rather stay in a job they don't like than have to go through the rejection of interviews.

So what happens is, we take what we can get so we don't have to face that inevitable rejection letter.

When we settle for second best, we might position our worth at the bottom of the scale. You may take a job you can get instead of one that you really wanted because of the chance they would refuse you. You get into a relationship with someone who treats you badly, but you don't leave because your self-esteem has convinced you that this is what you deserve. You could spend your life settling for anything that you can get instead of what you really want, or deserve.

Now, what if you could change this right now? What if, instead of settling for second best or just anything that comes your way, you choose to go after what you want instead of what you can get. Instead of settling, you raise the bar and decide right now to live by a set of new standards. Instead of going for what is easy, you go for what is right. Instead of giving into comfort and playing it safe, you will take a little risk and feel okay with it.

How different would your life be if you approached the subject of rejection from another angle? We know that getting rejected is something we can't avoid. It is a part of life. The people who embrace it as a necessary obstacle are the people that reach the summit, while everyone else is stuck at the base of the mountain, clambering for a foothold on a difficult climb.

The act of being rejected has power only when we feed it. By this, I mean if you accept everything that you don't want, you'll be left with the unwanted scraps that nobody else needed.

Your choices right now will open up a different door for you to walk through. You can change your satisfaction, fulfillment, and confidence levels the moment you make a higher choice for yourself, as soon as you decide that you will take the high road for a change.

What is a decision you could make right now that would prompt you to move in a new direction? How about raising your standards? Make a change to your personal value system?

Many times, we want to change but we stick with the same standards that get us nowhere. Stuck in jobs we don't like, relationships that make us sick, or living in an area that isn't suitable.

While it is important to choose what we want in life, it is equally important to identify with what we don't want.

Raise Your Standards

When you make an intentional decision on the things that you will no longer tolerate, from yourself and others, it changes everything. You could remove your core rejection issues overnight if you made a decision about what you deemed acceptable.

In most cases, we lower our values and thus lower our personal standards just so we can fit in. It is a form of people pleasing: you accept whatever people throw at you because you believe that is what you're worth.

By raising standards across the board, you find yourself making higher-level decisions that bring you greater opportunity. Would you feel sensitive if someone ignored you if your standards were raised? You'd think, "Fine, I'll find someone better." You can shift your entire perspective right now, today, by making a conscious decision on what you will no longer accept.

Will you let someone talk down to you without standing up for yourself?

Will you accept criticism from yourself if you don't succeed?

Will you continue to allow yourself to believe that you are unworthy or unlovable?

Right now, you are going to make a list of the beliefs, behaviors and attitudes that you no longer accept. This list has two parts.

1. What I no longer accept from myself.

2. What I no longer accept from other people.

You can divide your list up into the various areas of your life such as relationships, work, friends, personal values, and social situations.

Once you can identify what you don't want, you can focus on what you do want. For example, if someone you know treats you badly, set the standards for what you will accept from this person. Be honest with them. Call them out when they put you down or act inappropriately. If they don't change, you can leave.

Take action when something goes against your raised standards. For whatever it's worth, do not lower your standards to please someone else. If you do, you'll be back where you started.

Chapter Recap

Look for moments in your day-to-day life that you choose to do something out of fear. Did you agree to do something for fear of being frowned on? Were you intimidated to speak for fear of being ridiculed? Rejection is a cycle that can hold us back. Instead of being our true selves, we hide in the shadows from shame.

Look for the good in rejection. There is an upside to rejection that we often fail to see. Instead of a villain that we should avoid, think of it as a necessary companion always there to help you move forward, even if this means progress is painful.

Be aware of how you react to the moods of others. When they are angry or being overly controlling or demanding, is your fear on high alert? Are you ready to agree with anything they say just to get along? If you are overly sensitive to the environment when it is hostile, you may try to 'get along' to avoid being targeted. But if this is the case, you'll always resort to people-pleasing.

In the end, we want to base our choices in life, not out of fear but by asking ourselves this one question: "Am I taking action based on my values? Is this the right thing to do?"

Dealing with rejection is a learning curve. Take it head on and embrace the lesson it has to teach.

Moving into the next chapter we will learn about shifting the negative beliefs so we can deal with our feelings of inferiority and destroy limited thinking patterns.

Chapter 5

Shifting Negative Beliefs

"If you don't have solid beliefs, you cannot build a stable life. Beliefs are like the foundation of a building, and they are the foundation to build your life upon."

— **Alfred A. Montapert**

In this chapter, I am going to cover the limiting beliefs you may have about yourself and how to convert these to positive beliefs. We can accomplish this in five simple steps that I'll cover later.

The core of an inferiority mindset begins with the negative beliefs that have damaged a person's self-esteem and devalued their worth. In order to be free and build a life of better quality, making a shift in just one of our beliefs can have tremendous impact on our emotions and thoughts.

When you disengage the beliefs keeping you trapped, it frees up space for healthier beliefs to create a new operating system. As long as our limiting beliefs convince us that something is wrong with us, the negative cycle continues to repeat itself.

This negativity cycling is how we stay stuck: By re-living the same behaviors and focusing on damaging, worn-out thoughts day in and day out. When we focus on replacing our faulty beliefs, we can start to shift away from the inferiority persona and move towards building a more positive outlook.

Belief Limitations Exposed

Negative core beliefs express lies about who we are and what we can do. These are supported by a thousand distorted thoughts and corrupt ideas working together to support the false statements we have come to believe in.

Whereas destructive beliefs can ruin us, a system of positive beliefs focused on building confidence will generate a system of healthier thoughts and boost our self-esteem and confidence.

Negative beliefs are the cracks in character that need to be mended if any kind of long-term success is to be achieved. The causes of these beliefs extend into past childhood events as well as life experiences that we linked our pain to.

For example, if you experienced rejection as a child from a parent per se, you may have formed the internal beliefs that you are unlovable and therefore not worthy of love or acceptance. This conditioned belief also lends to hypersensitivity, as we covered in the previous chapter.

Remember:

Your beliefs have had a lifetime to grow and form deep roots within your conscious and subconscious mind.

While directing our lives based on the false perception of our past reality, we limit our chances for any kind of real growth or personal development. But it is not necessary to go back and dig up all of our old skeletons.

We can start from where we are today. Regardless of how a belief was created or why, we can focus on the NOW. The past is not your future. How you perceive an event makes it a lesson learned or a painful experience you choose not to repeat.

You can implement five steps to reverse the way you have been thinking, believing, and behaving. You can change these beliefs to work for you instead of against you. The goal here is to identify and discard the beliefs you have that don't support you, while shifting towards a set of new beliefs to empower your life.

Many of your beliefs about yourself are lies that have been reinforced since childhood. Once we integrate a belief we rarely question it but come to accept it as the way things are.

By choosing to develop more empowering beliefs that support and build the way of life you desire to have, you can create a detailed map for success that guides you to the places you wish to go. You are creating your reality, as you want it, instead of just passively accepting the way things are.

Whatever your current state is, you can change that in an instant. Earlier we talked about raising your standards so that the rejection you have been sensitive to can no longer hurt you. By deciding what we will no longer take, and then deciding what is acceptable, we can shift the beliefs that are managing our current state.

The Six-Step Process for Changing a Belief

You can pull yourself out of the current state you're in if you don't want to be there. You can shift your emotions to be positive and create more optimism in your life. With this in mind, a chosen system of thoughts that empower you also leads to the development of an empowering belief system.

Step 1: Identify the belief you want to change. Identifying the beliefs you want to change is the first step to taking positive action and doing something about it. You can only change something if you know what you need to change and why you want to change it.

Core negative beliefs that are making you feel inferior, inadequate, and worthless should be first on your list. Why hang on to your painful thoughts any longer? This is a tough step for most people. We have been feeding into our pain for so long it starts to appear normal.

I can assure you that in working through your pain, and recognizing the negative beliefs you created about yourself, your life starts to take a dramatic shift.

Here are some examples of the beliefs you may have about yourself. See if you recognize any of these:

"Everything bad that happens to me is my fault."

"I feel like I am less competent than everybody else when it comes to success or getting ahead in life."

"I feel like a failure or a 'nobody' when in the presence of other people who are obviously better than me."

"I have no qualities worth talking about that anyone would be interested in."

"I should be perfect at all times. I have to show people I am perfect."

"I am inherently flawed."

"I am inferior to everyone else. They are smarter, more educated, and seem to land on their feet when all I do is fail from day to day."

"I'm no good, and everybody knows it."

"Once someone gets to know me, they will just leave me like everybody else."

"My family was extremely dysfunctional; so, I am dysfunctional."

"If only she would stop treating me that way, I'd feel better about this situation and myself."

You might have a number of faulty beliefs about yourself that have disempowered you throughout most of your life. I know I did before I worked to turn them around. The key is to recognize what they are. Some are buried deep. Others are more noticeable and are running through your mind on automatic pilot a hundred times a day. They feel so normal that you do not question their validity.

Take time to write them out and list as many as you can. You can start with parts of the short list above that apply and add to it with your own negative beliefs. Pay attention to the beliefs that target your self-esteem and devalue your worth.

Step 2: Disempower the old belief by injecting doubt and uncertainty. In this next step you want to inject doubt and uncertainty into the equation. It is time to take a stand and question your belief thoroughly, analyzing it under a mental microscope through strict analysis. It is time to put your beliefs on trial.

You are going to question your beliefs, attacking their vulnerability, tearing down their walls, and weakening their structure. If a belief has been built on lies and falsehoods, it will not stand up to the scrutiny of your attack.

Here is an example:

"My family was extremely dysfunctional; so, I am dysfunctional."

Using this as an example, let's take a look. Begin by questioning this belief. Act as if you are actually interrogating this belief. Talk back to it; talk down to it. Take away its power. Make a decision to reject this as any truth.

Here is an example of what I wrote:

"What is the basis for this belief?"

"My family life was not perfect by any means. My parents loved me conditionally and they had their own issues to deal with. Many times I felt rejected or outcast. But this does not mean that I am dysfunctional. To a degree, isn't everyone? Don't we all struggle with our own defects? I refuse to accept this belief anymore."

Go deep with your ideas and push back hard. Then, ask pertinent questions that disengage the power your belief has over you. Put your belief on trial! Tell yourself that this is not a reality you choose to believe in anymore. Disown it completely. Choose to believe in something else. This decision to have a new belief is when your mind makes a shift towards reframing what it has been trained to accept.

Step 3: Reframe the new belief while discarding the old one. When reframing a new belief, the key is to convince ourselves it is real. We have to believe it! This is difficult to do when we start out. Full of fear, self-doubt, and lacking in confidence, we can easily fall back into old patterns of defeat. We can convince ourselves that the negative belief (I am no good because I always fail, so why bother) is true.

When you decide to replace your old beliefs, you are making a firm commitment: *I refuse to feel this way anymore. From now on I am going to believe this about myself and reject all negative thoughts that try to enter my mind.* If you do this enough over the course of days and weeks to come you will be thinking and behaving differently.

Now...

Step 4: Visualize the person you will become once you have created that new belief. Visualize yourself behaving differently. Visualize taking new and decisive actions, and pushing through your fear instead of being blocked by it. See yourself overcoming your inferiority complex by living life in a more vigorous way.

Step 5: Reinforce the new belief, taking further repetitive action toward making it real. Now that you have a solid idea of the changes you want, start by supporting your new belief. Take immediate action and reframe your old belief with the new one.

If you tear down the old belief but do nothing to replace it, when difficult times come up (and they will) you will resort to that old destructive way of thinking again. When this happens, just remember what your replacement belief is and continue to reinforce it over and over. Such reinforcement has to be done consistently in order to succeed.

One way to take action on this is to write out ten of your favorite quotes. Utilize the power of positive words. From there you can move onto positive affirmations. Repeat these several times a day. It will be uncomfortable at first, but be persistent.

The more you use words of positive power, the faster you can shift your beliefs to accepting what you are saying and thinking. Persistence and consistency are the keys. Keep at it. Soon you will be able to pull out your positive mental toolbox and use it to overpower those negative thoughts and words that punish.

Self-conversation is a powerful tool. Your negative beliefs used this tool against you for many years. Now you know that you can choose thoughts that support your new belief. Give your new belief lots of encouragement and support. Repeat it as many times as you need to. Convince yourself that it is true!

Step 6: Follow Up Action. In this final stage, you are going to continually strengthen your belief through convincing evidence. You will also alter your actions and behaviors to align with the new belief as it starts to plant its roots deep into your subconscious.

A belief responds to action and confirmation that what it is experiencing through your thoughts and actions is your reality.

It is important to follow up your reinforcement of the new beliefs on a continual basis. Create the beliefs you want to have. Do not settle on or accept the thoughts that devalue you.

Once a year, you could give yourself a small test to see where you are at with your beliefs and, analyze whether they are consistent with your desires and purpose.

You may discover, as I have, that there are new discrepancies with your current beliefs and values. If so, you can always update your belief system every year, making subtle changes here and there, adjusting your course in order to stay on track.

Keep Track of Your Empowering Beliefs

We have a lot of faulty beliefs about ourselves. I am referring to those beliefs that do not accurately represent who we are. We buy into these false messages because our belief system has been conditioned and tricked into thinking this is real, and this is who I am.

Buying in to these inaccurate beliefs is false conditioning. We must observe our behavior and the thoughts and beliefs that are driving it. The beliefs that feed us those negative messages sound like truths, but they are the lies we must replace.

I recommend that you keep track of both **empowering** and **disempowering** beliefs in a notebook. On one side, write down the beliefs that you want to change; these are your disempowering beliefs. On the other side, write down the positive beliefs that empower you.

An example of a disempowering belief would be:

"I'll never succeed at this. I'll always be poor because I can't save money."

An empowering belief, however, could be:

"I can earn as much money as I want when I build the business I have been dreaming of."

Negative beliefs keep you stuck, and hold you back from pushing forward. Positive beliefs build up your self-esteem and confidence. They stimulate your mind to snap to action and get unstuck. Work to focus on the beliefs that are helping you to succeed.

We should take some time out to observe what we are thinking. The best time for this is when we find ourselves in a situation when we feel rejected. This could be when our confidence is challenged, someone is criticizing us, or we feel the urge to counterattack.

Chapter Recap

We have just looked at the limiting beliefs that formed our rejectionist mindset. Disengage these beliefs and we are well on our way to defeating any situation where you feel inferior or that your personal worth is being scrutinized. Be patient and give it time.

As I suggested, make lists of both negative and positive beliefs. Read them both out loud. Cross out the disempowering beliefs and focus on the positive ones. Use positive quotes and affirmations to support positive thinking and action, and work them into framing a new mindset.

Now, let's move into the next chapter right away because I am going to cover the cycle of rejection. I will show you the process and pattern that starts working when you are in a situation that causes you to feel inferior.

Now you can listen to the audiobook version of Rejection Reset on Audible.

If so, you can try the Audible 30-day free trial.
To get access:
1. Go to audible.com (or.de/.uk)
2. Type in "Scott Allan"
3. Click the orange button "free with 30-day trial" on the right side of the audiobook.
4. Enjoy the audiobook version of **Rejection Reset!**

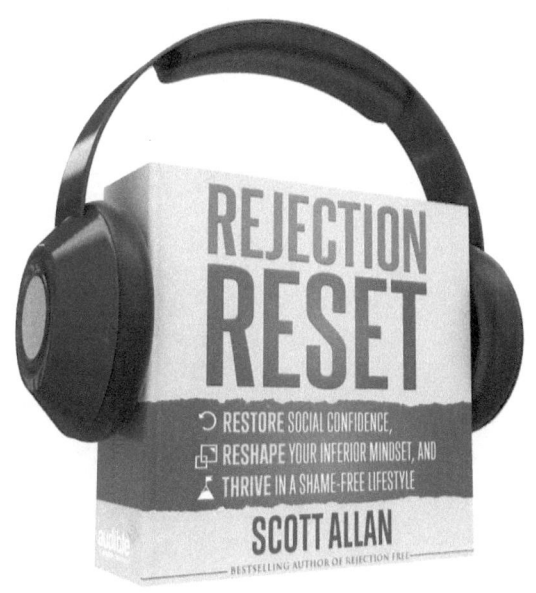

Chapter 6

The Cycle of Rejection

"People tend to dwell more on negative things than on good things. So the mind then becomes obsessed with negative things, with judgments, guilt and anxiety produced by thoughts about the future and so on."

— **Eckhart Tolle**

In the last chapter you gained some good insight on how to change negative beliefs about yourself. Now, I am going to show you the cycle that accompanies the rejection mindset.

This is the painful pattern of defeat that has been formed over years of conditioning. In this chapter I will go through each of the stages to give you a clear idea what happens when you choose to be rejected in any situation.

The condition of feeling inferior and inadequate can be best explained in the cycle that keeps the condition active. Our goal, as you will see in this book, is to deactivate the cycle you are currently using and then replace it with a healthier cycle.

Why Change is Difficult

Change is difficult because people do the same things over and over again expecting different results. Einstein and other philosophers once described this as, "the definition of insanity."

If you want a different result, you have to do things in a different manner than you have been doing them. This includes habit change or shifting your beliefs and thoughts to react and behave differently than before.

Einstein also said: *"You can't solve a problem at the same level that it was created."*

Frustration sets in when you have the desire to make a change, such as to stop acting out in ways that reinforces your negative behavior, but the same feelings of inadequacy continue to prevail when we engage in the same behavior that keeps us in a rut.

For change to be successful, you have to reframe your reality. This new reality is going to be your new constructive pattern to replace the old destructive one. Instead of acting out the old ways, you are going to replace these with new healthy behaviors that move you away from the old you. It is not easy, but I can show you a way that worked for many others and me.

Basically, the cycle of defeat that we create when our sense of rejection is triggered looks like this:

1. An internal trigger is "switched on" by external events or conditions.
2. A pain point is activated.
3. A faulty choice is made based on previous experience.
4. An escape tactic or coping mechanism is initiated.
5. There is a result that has a favorable outcome/conclusion.
6. The cycle is repeated, or the result, such as escaping from our pain, is achieved and a faulty conclusion is reached.

Breaking Down the Steps

An internal trigger is switched on: When you experience a situation that is stressful and causes anxiety or fear, a trigger is activated by an external event. Trigger activation could be brought on by familiar situations connected to childhood trauma or circumstances that trigger feelings of loneliness, depression, or anger.

The resulting action could be to act out defensively or engage in compulsive behavior to minimize the internal pain. The trigger is what happens first; the action you choose to deal with it is selected by the nature of the pain point experienced.

A pain point is activated: I will talk about pain points in more detail shortly. The initial trigger that sets us off activates our various pain points. In most cases it is driven by the shame-based persona.

Pain points can be feelings of vulnerability, defectiveness, rejection, failure, or abandonment that act as our primary switch and determine what we will do next. A pain point is experienced when a situation comes up that triggers stress, anxiety or fear. Based on this, we choose a self-defeating behavior to cope with the situation.

A faulty choice is made based on previous experience: We choose to behave or respond using a technique that masks the pain. Who wants to feel those things when we can hide or control it using a coping strategy?

When choices are made by default, they are performed automatically without thought or analysis of the conclusions that we end up with. It is our default choice. At the time, we might think we have no other choice, but we do. We convince ourselves we have no other options so that we have an excuse to act out without taking responsibility for the consequences.

There is real power in our choices when we decide with a mind that is fully switched on. When we fall back on default choices, we give up our power to take charge and just let things happen to us instead of taking control. Responsibility only comes to those who have earned it.

A technique is chosen based on either escape or coping strategy: Once a pain point has been activated we have to choose an avoidance technique; this is a coping strategy that enables us to deal with the situation by choosing an action that works to eliminate or numb out fear and anxiety. The type of and degree of behavior chosen depends on the level of pain or discomfort you feel.

We can counterattack and defend, possibly by using an addiction such as alcohol, sex, or binge eating. Or, we might turn into a critical monster and start tearing someone down as soon as they are not around. Escape tactics and coping strategies focus on short-term solutions that eventually fail. They have a goal to help us escape but really, the end result is further denial and isolation.

Expected outcome relieves tension, frustration, or stress; a conclusion is drawn that proves our faulty beliefs.

After applying the coping strategy that focuses on escaping or avoidance, the predicted outcome results and tension and anxiety are relieved at least until the next trigger.

And then…

The cycle reinforces and repeats.

During the rejection cycle a pattern is followed that leads to a repetition of damaging choices, which solidifies the behavior. In a situation in which we feel vulnerable, fearful, or totally defective, the obvious choice is to either cope with it or escape from it.

This pattern is the core of our coping strategy, and it keeps our negative beliefs, emotions, and thoughts working to support our false reality. This reality is an illusion that we continue to buy into.

Failure Expectation and the Escape Plan

When the 'fear of rejection' switch is triggered, there is an automatic reaction to deal with the emotional pain that's coming. This switch could be triggered by the fear of a job interview, talking to people we are attracted to, or public speaking.

Whatever the situation is, there is a level of anxiety experienced. It is this initial nervousness that starts the process and we then buy into a certain falsehood associated with the situation or event.

We begin to visualize what could happen if our voice cracks or we lose confidence. We see ourselves failing and feel others watching us and judging. All of these fears build up. We then enter the situation, expecting to be rejected, judged, or looked down on at some level. In other words, we are expecting the failure we know is coming. By choosing this expectation at an unconscious level we manifest the failure or rejection.

The purpose of this cycle is avoidance and escape. Rather than cope with a situation we are not prepared to handle, we choose the default path. It is the only option when we believe that nothing else exists, and that there is no other way out.

Let's say our escape route is an addiction such as drinking or eating junk food. When we have stress or pressure brought on by a situation that we decide we cannot face up to or control, our pain point is activated and fear-based thoughts choose the path of least resistance (an addiction) to cope with the situation.

When we feed into the action by either filling up on junk food or wanting to get drunk, we escape the pain of facing reality. This has a good conclusion based on a distorted reality.

You see, this cycle is self-defeating, yet we recreate it and tap into it whenever a fear-based situation or problem comes up. The reaction is to "get out of the house before it burns down."

Many people had to deal with some painful emotions as a child when they were abandoned, felt inadequate, or were criticized. Having no say in this, they formed a coping mechanism that molded into the only way out for them.

The **escape plan** is the way out; it is their back door to a survival mechanism that promised to relive the emotional pain. In reality, it becomes a box that keeps them trapped. For many people, they spend decades locked in this turbulent cycle that has no end.

We are going to work at shifting your perception so that you see yourself through a different lens. Imagine if you were to look through a telescope on one end and then turn it around and look through the other end. The view is different.

Your aim is to shift your view of the world. You have to set your own expectations so that you do not fall victim to a cycle of defeat. Your goal is to break the pattern of reacting to the pain point by engaging in healthy techniques that diminish anxiety and fear through healthy choices.

Now, there are two paths we can take when dealing with diminishing fear and anxiety. One path is the escape plan. Our pain point is triggered; we want to avoid pain, so, by natural default, our habit is to activate a technique (defeat strategy) to deal with pain reduction.

The selected addiction path looks like the best choice, but, in reality, it is the path to failure. We may experience the momentary relief of evading the fear and pain but, in the end, it just drives us into further seclusion. An example would be an addiction or faulty behavior such as lying, exaggerating, or trying to impress others.

The other path, the positive self-talk one, is the path of courage. It is the goal we are going to achieve here. When we take this high road, we feel the fear and push through it anyway instead of taking the easy way and fleeing.

We are willing to feel what is happening. Instead of choosing by default, we take the way out of the pain by choosing a healthier way of responding. This is the conscious choice. The way to be courageous is to do the thing that you fear the most. Take action when you are afraid.

A cycle is only broken when different choices are made followed by a new course of action. The reward you get from going through the grit is far more fulfilling than sticking to what has always worked and what has always failed you.

Learned Behavior & Framed Reality

Nobody is born inadequate or flawed. Character defects are a part of life, but when we act out using strategies to control our defects, we make them stronger.

In the case of rejectionism, our aim in the "Cycle of Defeat," is to avoid feeling rejected. There are several ways we can do this. For example: criticizing others before they get to us, retaliate by destroying someone else's reputation, or isolating ourselves from a group to get away from the risk of looking stupid or being exposed.

The bottom line is shame: We are afraid that someone is going to find out our dirty little secret and then the party is over. Our ego will do anything to prevent this.

As a child we may have been injured in some way; we had no defense. As an adult living in the big world, everything is exposed for the world to see. But at our core, that injured child still seeks retribution; it wants an apology or nothing at all.

We have framed our reality around protecting this child. It is a fear-based reality, but it demands our attention at all times. We are on guard constantly. And, when we keep a close vigil to protect what is ours, the Cycle of Defeat becomes our strategy. Now we are going to work at changing this strategy and replacing it with a new one.

The new cycle is designed to replace the old one, almost how we would switch out the parts in a car. It can be done, and the process is similar. We have seen the cycle that plays out when a situation or individual threatens our ego.

In order to cope with the threat, action has to be taken; this action, up to this point, has been a negative cycle of defeat that led to a favorable result that reduced anxiety or made us feel less uncomfortable. But it is a faulty system based on escape. We are not dealing with anything; we are sweeping the problem under the rug.

Chapter Recap

Be aware of your internal triggers. When you experience a situation that is stressful and causes anxiety or fear, a trigger is activated by an external event.

Pain points, such as feelings of vulnerability, defectiveness, rejection, failure, or abandonment, act as our primary switch and determine what we will do next.

We use various coping strategies, such as counterattacking, to deal with our unresolved issues to mask the pain.

A faulty choice is made based on previous experience: We choose to behave or respond using a technique that masks the pain.

We can respond to your rejection in two ways: Fight or flee. We can escape or take courage and do something about it. A cycle is only broken when different choices are made followed by a new course of action.

You can change by framing a new reality for yourself.

"Authors by the hundreds can tell you stories by the thousands of those rejection slips before they found a publisher who was willing to 'gamble' on an unknown."

— **Zig Ziglar**

Chapter 7

The Breakthrough Cycle

"Between stimulus and response there is a space. In that space is our power to choose our response. In our response lies our growth and our freedom."

— **Victor E. Frankl,** Auschwitz survivor and author of *Man's Search for Meaning*

With some simple strategies and solutions you can learn to confront your inner demons. You can develop greater courage to talk to them, push them out of the way, and charge forward without being held back.

Our goal is to disempower the beliefs that are slowing you down and keeping you stuck, because in the end, that is all they are: **obstacles**. They are not permanent barriers, but they do rob you of your personal power over time if not treated.

As we will see, you can choose to engage in the empowering thoughts, actions and behaviors that serve you best. You can rise above the barriers of personal self-defeat and tap into that inner strength that you know is there.

Making Choices That Matter

Let's take a look at making choices. When we find ourselves in a situation that threatens our self-esteem, or could expose us to shame, a survival mechanism kicks in. We unconsciously make a decision to take action to prevent exposing our pain point.

Our thoughts, wired into this cycle, are fearful like animals that flee from fire. Our thoughts are directed toward self-preservation. We will do anything to avoid being humiliated or have our flaws exposed. Seeing our flaws under a "social microscope" is one of our big fears.

When it comes to making an empowering choice, we choose poorly. That is to say, we choose the path that alleviates the pain. This is usually a coping strategy that has been tested again and again, and based on the reward gained from using this strategy, this appears to be the logical choice.

One technique, or "escape strategy plan," is to engage in some behavior that forces you to make a choice. This choice is made, in most cases, through acting out and just letting it happen passively. We need to be intentional about our choices if they are to have any long-term impact.

Think about a choice you have made in the past that was made with intention. How did you come to make it? Was it based on relevant information? Did you make the choice after considering other options? Was the choice successful or did it lead to a bad result?

Choices based on intentional effort have a high probability of achieving a successful outcome. When you choose unconsciously (without any logical thinking or reasoning), you have little to do with controlling the outcome, and in making a decision based on your fearful emotions you end up taking a lower path that you will later regret. This eventually becomes a repetitive cycle that we fall into.

This can occur through a psychological process known as repetition compulsion, where we unconsciously repeat the same painful experiences over and over again. If being rejected and feeling like "a nobody" is a normal experience, it could become natural to continue reliving this same experience over and over.

Breaking the Cycle

In everything you do there are choices. If you choose path A, you will get that. Choose path B, you get something else [will you take the red pill or the blue one?]. Sometimes what you might get is a surprise you were least expecting, but if you keep doing the same thing over and over, the surprise turns to expectation based on the result and conclusion of previous "experiments."

Like a bad habit that delivers the same outcome, there is no surprise left. We know what to expect from engaging in the same behaviors repeatedly. This is why we need a new set of actions to create a better cycle. Over the years we may have developed a pattern of bad results that continue to reinforce the cycle of defeat that feeds into the inferiority complex.

You can end this all right now.

Instead of feeling worthless, you decide your worthiness. Instead of rejecting yourself, learn to love yourself and all your faults. Instead of comparing yourself to other people who have more, try to see life as an abundant opportunity. Up until now, you have been living with less; now we are going to focus on building abundance and a higher quality lifestyle through six simple steps.

The Six-Step Process for Creating Lasting Change

Here is the six-step process you can implement right away and start to see immediate results.

1. Identify the behavior you want to change. Admitting that you are not perfect is a big step. When you admit that something in your life is not working, you set the stage to make it work.

Here is an example: After taking time to observe my behavior, I knew that one of my character defects was trying to impress others. I would brag about things I was working on, made myself sound smarter and more confident, and implied that I had big things going on. I wanted people who had what I wanted to recognize me as an equal. I was seeking validation and acceptance. If I did not get it, I would feel rejected and worthless.

Looking for external validation from others could be setting yourself up for a let-down. Your sense of value is riding on their opinions, most of which are not based on facts, but driven by emotions. A person's perception of you can, and will, change from day to day. The only true validation you need is your own.

Seeing this was a major breakthrough. When I admitted that this behavior was driving people away and not drawing them to me, I caught myself in the pattern. I could actually see when I was trying to impress others. Gradually, by stopping this behavior before it happened, I reduced the amount of times I did this. This allowed me to be honest, forthcoming, and more down-to-earth.

2. Make a decision today to change this behavior. Until you decide what it is you want, nothing happens. If you say, "Someday, I'll get around to it," that day will come five years later, and you will still be stuck.

Make a decision right now and stick with it. Choose to have a different outcome. Believe in what you have yet to discover. Turn your actions into conscious choices instead of actions based on default that inevitably lead to failure tearing away at your self-esteem and confidence.

Making this decision is something you have to reinforce again and again. Make your decision to focus on small changes every day. Keep at it and do not give up. Make a decision—everyday—that you are going to overcome any obstacle that stands in your way. This includes your limited beliefs, doubts, and fears that crop up.

3. Decide what you are willing to do to change. What are you willing to do? What will you have to give up in order to successfully implement these changes? What old behaviors are you struggling to let go of? What will be the price you pay if you do not make concessions?

These are important questions. There are many times when people want to change something (a bad habit or an obstacle) but, when it comes to paying the price, they start to negotiate. They want to change, but they soon realize nothing comes for free. To have the one thing we really desire usually requires surrendering something else. The things you insist on holding on to could be the same vices keeping you trapped.

When you are ready to pay the price in full, you will. By letting go gradually you can have everything you have ever wanted: peace of mind, stronger relationships, and a healthier frame of mind.

4. Choose a new response and action. What action is needed to implement changes right now? Is it a shift in your attitude? An addiction you are holding onto? Letting go of your attachment to a negative behavior? When you become willing to do whatever it takes, when you go all in with a full commitment to paying the price, your resistance towards creating new behavior loses its power and is broken down.

The reason most people struggle is because they are holding on too tight while still uncertain if they want to pay that price. But what does this mean? What are you going to pay? More importantly, what are you willing to give up?

Do you want to change your feelings of inferiority but still criticize others because it feels good or empowers you? Will you give up your defensiveness or keep it because you never know when you are going to need it?

Whenever you feel stuck and you are looking for a way to get out, remember that change always follows action. When you take intentional action towards your objectives you condition yourself to fear less and do more.

You may make mistakes, but nobody ever failed who put in an honest effort to push ahead and make a situation better. By staying focused on what you really want and by working continuously on improving your situation, you are taking a first step toward something much bigger.

5. Be ready for setbacks. It is important to be realistic. Nothing comes easily and more often than not you have to try at something several times before it works. This is the reason why, when you experience a setback or fall back into old patterns of defeat, it is important that you don't beat yourself up.

Not everything happens according to plan. What matters is that we have a good idea of the direction we want to take. Only then can we intentionally decide the right course of action to move towards that goal.

6. Continue to repeat and reinforce your success. This system works best when you take immediate action, recognize what is working best, and analyze the results you got so you can continue to fine-tune your strategy. If you do not succeed right away, keep working at it and continually reinforce your positive habits.

Repeat those positive actions that bring about the desired outcome and put an end to the behaviors that are dragging you down. After putting this cycle into practice, you will be able to recognize clearly how to act instead of react, how to choose instead of letting it happen by default, and how to be yourself instead of living a lie.

This is the essence of gaining freedom: When you are empowering your life by choice, learning by trial and error, doing what works, and eliminating the rest.

Chapter Recap

Now that you know how to use the new cycle to create change, be sure to implement it when your issues with rejection are challenged.

Always remember that nobody can reject you. Only you can do it to yourself. And now that you have the know-how to take action, there is nothing stopping you.

When I started to implement positive strategies into my life I could sense the *self-saboteur* within wanting to take back control. After repeating the positive cycle that begins with a conscious choice to get well, the negative side that wanted to ruin it all faded away.

When I experienced those feelings of inferiority I chose not to believe it. In choosing, you become empowered. And when this happens, any other barrier that stands in your way collapses.

Chapter 8

The Social Trigger Response

"Every time I thought I was being rejected from something good, I was actually being re-directed to something better."

— Dr. Steve Maraboli

A trigger response is a person, place, or situation that kicks our fear of rejection into taking action and reacting [out of fear] to a fearful situation. We feel compelled to act out in a destructive way. This is done by using an escape tactic to deal with a painful or fearful moment. Before we decide on the escape tactic to use, there has to be something happening that will trigger you to react.

Activating Trigger Responses

So, what is a trigger response? It is what sends an alcoholic back to drinking when seeing people having a good time in a bar. It is when a smoker will return to the habit when engaged in a situation where people are smoking.

It is when a social situation triggers feelings of shame when someone points out one of your flaws. It is when pressure in a social environment could trigger your rejectionist fears and trigger you to feel anxious or suddenly lose all confidence.

Our trigger responses could be activated by any one of the following situations:

- *Meeting people for the first time.*

- *Negative thoughts or "bad" thinking.*
- *Revisiting memory spots from your past.*
- *A situation that triggers a painful past experience.*
- *Hanging around with people who have more than you do, such as money, popularity, a nice car, or a family.*
- *Exposure to an addiction that once had fulfilling rewards.*
- *A demanding relationship.*
- *An overpowering boss or someone who demeans or criticizes you.*

Any one of these trigger points could cause you to react. Our triggers are defense mechanisms designed to protect us. Or so we are led to believe. But what they really function as is low-level trigger points. Instead of seeking a higher end solution, we buy into the easy path that usually turns into an escape route.

Emotional triggers are danger points because they rob us of all our hard work. Maybe you spent weeks or months trying to get through your emotional baggage, and then, wham! Next thing you know, you are confronted with a situation that compels you to act out. This makes you take action on something you'll later regret.

Remember that nobody can set us off. I often hear people complain that he or she really "set me off" or "my boss really gets on my nerves". But did they really? Are we not in control of our own emotions? Is someone forcing us to feel this way?

We are in control of our own emotional state at all times. Nobody can make us feel or do anything without our permission. It just seems that way when we lose control and convince ourselves we have no choice and so, we resort to taking negative action to get back at those people who are out to get us.

The Trigger and Emotion

The trigger is what sets us off, the switch is the emotion that it triggers (defensiveness, anger), and the technique through escape and coping strategy is the action we resort to in dealing with it. This is what is known in addiction recovery as a slip. And slips are to be expected in any kind of healing process.

Our intention here is to be aware of the situations, people, or places that we feel rejected by, and the stress connected to our past events. In many cases it is our interactions with people, but it can also be a place that has some memory attached to it. Our trigger is the first step to acting out against our pain point.

The Trigger in Action

We do not have to react to every situation or person that triggers us to act out. We do have a choice. When we are switched on against a trigger pattern, we may think that doing something, such as binge eating, as a way of coping with our emotions, is somehow going to make us feel better.

In the short run, we treat our pain by slipping back into our old ways. But in the long run, we continue to reinforce our escape route. The habit to escape and avoid our pain, while it feels like the right thing to do, is what keeps us stuck where we are.

When a trigger is activated for the rejectionist, he or she will start to go through a learned process. On the inside, they start to rationalize and feed into the condition. This could be unleashing verbal self-abuse, focusing on a negative thought pattern, making comparisons, or taking part in self-sabotaging actions that further support inferiority beliefs.

People have their favorite trigger techniques that are activated when those situations arise, because when they are switched on the behavior that they have created as their default mechanism channels into a specific action.

Some people start to rationalize the situation and feel somehow entitled to act out. The trigger action becomes an excuse: "Well, he made me do it," or "I had no other choice." In rationalizing their behavior, they are then giving themselves permission to do something about it. They want to get even, by taking the "I'll show them," attitude.

When our pain point is exposed, the situation that caused this is the trigger, and how we deal with it is to apply an escape tactic, a coping mechanism, or a combination of both.

Someone could trigger our pain point of inferiority and vulnerability, but we are in control of our own emotions at any given moment. We decide how to respond, react, and what actions to take. Do not be deceived into believing that "they made me do it." Once we accept responsibility for own responses, we can turn the situation around by choosing to respond appropriately.

Controlling Your Reactions

Remember this: The problem is not what other people do or say but how we react to the situation. Someone you just met could start talking about their most recent achievement. This may come across to us as bragging or trying to show off. If you are sensitive to rejection because of issues with low self-esteem, this conversation could be perceived as a means to undermine your own accomplishments that are not as significant.

Your emotions turn to jealousy or envy, and these feelings can only destroy a potentially good relationship.

But is that what is really happening? Could it be that the other person is just celebrating an achievement they have been working towards for a long time?

Hypersensitivity puts us on edge. Our feelings of inadequacy become triggered by the situation. For example, when we are low in our self-esteem or hypersensitive to our own rejections, we might feel inferior to someone who has a higher education and more job opportunities than we have. Because we are so tuned into our fears of feeling less-than, every word becomes a put down.

We perceive ourselves as intended victims when in fact, the other person was merely trying to show off instead of attacking. In being able to rationalize this and walk yourself through the moment, you can start to rationalize your thinking right there and then. When you see that it is not about you at all, we become less fearful and gain a better understanding of why we feel the way we do.

If our pain point is jealousy, we tap into our feelings of anger and resentment. We may attack that person with our internal "verbal monster," or begin to backstab by telling others how much we "can't stand that snob" (labeling) as a means to defend ourselves (counterattack). Whatever our attack or defense may be, that is where we will also find our best solution to dealing with it.

By recognizing our defensive/offensive strategies that trigger us to respond, this is where we gain personal power over the situation. We can own up to, and recognize that it is our reaction to the situation that challenges the moment we are in.

You lose control the moment you react to an external situation. But if you stay grounded and focused on the moment you can control your urge to react. When we become reactionary, we are acting out of fear. Your fear creates anger or anxiety.

Everyone has his or her own trigger situations. It could be a certain type of character personality or a familiar situation that connects them to a past event. Recognizing what our triggers are before they happen is the key to preventing us from acting out and falling into the negative cycle of defeat.

Action Steps for Managing Trigger Responses

1. Make a list of people and events/situations that trigger you to feel inferior by activating your feelings of inadequacy.

People: Is there someone who sets you off? What is it about this person that sets you off? Are they constantly bragging about past accomplishments? Is it a type of personality that you don't get along with?

In any case, certain people will trigger you to react: a romantic relationship, a family member, co-workers, or someone you just met for the first time. Relationships are difficult. It is the most volatile area for rejectionists because of their need to compare and seek assurance that they are okay.

Make a list of the people who set you off. Then, next to each name state a reason why this person bothers you. What is it about this person? By writing it out and identifying it you can better manage the situation when it comes up again.

You will likely react or act out many times again, but, if you can see it happening, this puts you in a position to take positive action towards a healthy outcome as opposed to just reacting and hoping for the best.

Events or social functions: Do you dread social events? Is a certain type of event more challenging? If so, what is it that triggers your fear? What are the reasons? Is it because you fear not being able to measure up? Is your shame point going to be exposed? Do you have to give a speech? Are you afraid of attracting attention?

Action Step 1: Control Your Trigger Response

Make a list of the kind of social functions that set you off. Is it interacting with others? Do you feel the need to compare, or do you find yourself in counterattack situations? By recognizing this you can choose to:

1. Go into the situation with better strategies for dealing with it, or

2. Avoid these types of situations altogether.

Catch your trigger before it happens. Once you have identified your triggers, you will know when to expect them. You will still occasionally get caught off guard, but by making yourself aware of these, when it happens, you will be in a better position to deal with it.

By knowing beforehand what your triggers are, you can create strategies beforehand to stop yourself from acting out or feeling like a nobody. Talk to yourself in a positive way. Talk to others in a positive way. You can change your emotions by responding through choice.

Choose a different response. Using the substitution technique [Chapter 10], you can replace your tactics with new, positive techniques that are not self-defeating. You can choose how to deal with your emotion.

You should not disown or ignore your feelings by downplaying them and acting as if they don't matter. Your feelings are real, even if they are not what you want. But how you respond, how you choose to act, makes the difference. Instead of acting out in a perpetual "I'll show them!" attitude, do something for yourself.

Action Step 2: Do Something for Yourself

- Go the gym and have an amazing workout.

- Buy yourself something nice and spend an afternoon with friends talking through how you feel.

- Call someone and invite him or her to a movie or dinner.

- Set a goal and spend 30 minutes a day working on it.
- Take a trip you have always dreamed about.
- Invest in your education: Enroll in an online course or sign up for evening classes at university.

These are substitution techniques, and they are far better than the usual default tactics of lashing out and getting even.

Chapter Recap

Be aware of the situations, people, or places that we feel rejected by, and the stress connected to our past events. Trigger points are activated by a situation we have difficulty coping with.

When confronted by someone who triggers a bad memory from your past, you might respond out of fear. Your trigger point is a defense mechanism.

By recognizing our defensive/offensive strategies that trigger us to respond, this is where we gain personal power over the situation. We can recognize that it is our reaction to the situation that challenges the moment we are in.

By knowing beforehand what your triggers are, you can create strategies beforehand to stop yourself from acting out.

Here are the steps simplified:

1. Identify who and what your triggers are.
2. Catch your trigger before it happens.
3. Choose a different response.

The next chapter shows you how the pain points you experience connect to your triggers. By understanding the dynamics of this, you will be able to handle any difficult situation when it comes up.

Chapter 9

Confronting Pain Points

"Strength does not come from physical capacity. It comes from an indomitable will."

— **Mahatma Gandhi**

We are going to go deeper and talk about the internal pain points that are triggered when our internal defects are exposed. Before we can react with an escape strategy or coping mechanism, something has to trigger the cycle. That switch is the pain point. A pain point is what we experience when our sensitivity to rejection is triggered.

To elaborate on this, the trigger is the external situation, event, or person that sets off the cycle. The pain point is like an open wound that has never healed and is attracted to vulnerable situations that demand sympathy or attention. If you are not careful, tuning towards your pain point for instant relief could be setting you up for failure.

Selecting Coping Mechanisms

Your pain point is an emotional state triggered by an event or set of circumstances. For example, we can feel a sudden stab of jealousy if a friend shows up at a party with a date and we do not have one. Or someone we know has more money, more talent, more opportunity, and always seems to land on their feet while we struggle with everything.

When hit with a situation that challenges our self-esteem or social confidence, one or more of our pain points are triggered. When this happens, our default reaction is to choose an action that diminishes the emotional pain. This is when one of our coping mechanisms are chosen.

As a note to what is listed below, most people can have multiple coping mechanisms rather than just one.

Here are a few examples of how people cope with painful situations:

- A woman in an emotionally abusive relationship suffers from being rejected by her partner, and so she looks for a way out to be free of the situation.
- A man at work is ostracized by his coworkers, and he may want to find a quiet place of his own to do his work. These people can go weeks or months without talking to anyone.
- A boy is in a family situation where one or both of his parents reject him for not measuring up to their expectations. He becomes distant and retreats to his bedroom to avoid any negative communication or criticism.
- You are being compared to other people at work, and their evaluations are much higher than yours. You are told that you have to work harder to be at the same level as everyone else. Fearing that you might fail, you take care of the problem by quitting.
- During a speech you accidentally stutter or forget what you are going to say, and someone in the crowd laughs, exposing your shame-based fears and breaking all confidence. You quickly wrap-up the speech and leave the venue, vowing to never give a speech again.

Experiencing rejection is an isolating emotion that drives people to retreat, hide, and put up defensive barriers to keep the "ugly" people out. Detaching from a relationship eventually leads to a breakdown of the marriage or partnership. Detaching from people at work leads to poor employee relations. Detaching from family leaves a child feeling abandoned.

Handling these difficult emotions is disempowering when we have limited skills to deal with them. Let's take the example of the child who was rejected by their parents. This is someone who had love withheld as a child and may feel detached or vulnerable in his or her adult years. In a situation that triggers this pain point, they now look for a means to cope through practicing avoidance tactics.

When they have established an escape route (an addiction, counterattack, or detachment) it relieves the pressure of having to deal with their pain point.

Someone who tries to avoid feelings of vulnerability may jump from relationship to relationship and never commit to any one person. If a woman's pain point is anxiety or loneliness she may isolate and make excuses for not going out. Remember that at the core of every pain point the goal is to avoid being rejected or emotionally injured.

By avoiding what hurts, we invite more of it into our lives. By escaping from the pain that we have never dealt with, we keep it and help it to manifest itself. What we are going to do now is identify our core pain points.

We all have at least one primary pain point we deal with throughout life. Depending on the nature of the experience or condition that pain point will be connected to a favored escape strategy to numb or cope with the feelings you want to bury.

Here is a list of the most common pain points. This is the start of the cycle that we are looking at next. See if you experience any of these pain points:

- Jealousy
- Defectiveness
- Inferiority
- Isolation
- Guilt
- Vulnerability
- Shyness
- Exclusion
- Abandonment
- Chronic worry
- Shame
- Helplessness

It is natural to attach ourselves to the strongest pain point, and, when we attach ourselves to it emotionally we develop defensive strategies for dealing with it. For example, a man whose pain point is "vulnerability" may cheat on his wife or girlfriend; if it is jealousy, he may sabotage someone just to get even or criticize or demean someone just to feel better.

We all have a strategy that we implement at an unconscious level. It feels like it is a part of us, and so we may catch ourselves making excuses by saying "That's just me." But it is not us. It is what we do in defense to protect a fearful ego. It is a learned behavior, and they can be changed if we discipline ourselves to recognize these patterns of defeat as they occur.

The Shame-Based Persona

One of the most damaging core pain points is shame. It is at the center of our self-esteem issues, self-confidence, and social well-being. If you feel great shame in certain situations, you may try to impress people, please them, or go along with everyone just to avoid conflict. Feeling worthless and embarrassed may lead to you hating conversations because you do not know what to contribute or say.

Here are some symptoms of a shame-based mindset for someone we will call Sam:

1. Sam was made to feel guilty because problems that were experienced in the home were somehow his fault.

2. He was ignored, neglected, or abandoned by those who were supposed to love him the most.

3. He was rarely, if ever, praised for doing good but criticized for what he didn't do.

4. He didn't meet high expectations put on him, and he felt like a failure.

5. He was compared to other kids, even siblings, and would hear things like, "Now why can't you be more like that?"

6. He would hear his parents talk about other kids and how "smart and talented" they were, which meant he had no support or anyone in his corner.

7. He only felt normal when he could isolate himself and be alone.

8. He has panic attacks when he has to speak in public.

9. *He is constantly comparing himself to others and feeling less than with each comparison.*

10. *He needs reassurance from people: his boss, his partner, or his family.*

As an adult, because love was conditional and withheld, or not all of Sam's needs were met while growing up, there remains bitterness and cold anger. He wants what is owed to him and goes through life demanding it from others.

This drive to "get what he is owed" becomes a demand on others who see him as needy, selfish and overly dependent. Feeling ousted and indifferent, he develops a rejectionist mindset.

Sam's greatest fear is that somebody is going to find out who he is. His protective persona will be exposed. People are going to see right through him and the phoniness. His defects will be brought to light and there will be no place to hide. This is at the core of the shame-based mindset and the foundation for living with inferiority feelings.

Deep within us is a desire to be accepted, loved, and nurtured. Even as adults, these feelings never leave. But instead of seeking it from our parents, we now ask the world for it in our relationships and from complete strangers.

When we do not get it or if the other person cannot fulfill our demands or expectations we develop the victim attitude that says, "Oh, they don't care about me," or "Nobody understands me." These are faulty beliefs.

When you become a victim, you develop a helpless mindset built from fragile confidence that diminishes your sense of worth. This can transition into a form of learned helplessness: a condition where a person suffers from a sense of powerlessness, usually occurring from a traumatic event or a persistent failure to succeed.

As children, we were diminished by the successes we never had. They could have been from failing or never being able to measure up to our parents' unrelenting standards. The defects of those you trusted most were thrust on you. We did not know this at the time, but what we were expected to fulfill placed a heavy burden on us. And because of this, the fear and feelings of rejection becomes a part of us.

It lives within us and we are convinced that it is a part of us. When we have a lack of confidence, especially in engaging with others, we revert back to these feelings of inferiority. It is the automatic response.

Right now, let's focus on what you can do. I will leave this chapter with some action steps that you can take. I promise you that any action that moves you toward a stronger, healthier way of thinking and behaving is going to have a significant impact on the quality of your thoughts and emotions.

Over time, you can heal and learn to be whole again. You are already there; you just need some deep work to move closer towards that goal. It is far from perfection that we are striving for but small victories by overcoming our personal obstacles holding us down.

And give it enough time. Do not expect instant results; rather, focus on building your awareness one day at a time. And one day at a time your feelings of inadequacy and inferiority will become greatly diminished.

Action Steps

Revisit your shame-based childhood. The origin of shame stems from your family life. Someone criticized you or demeaned you. The love you wanted was conditional and not real. See yourself as an adult now revisiting this child. What would you say or do to comfort them?

Visualize this and comfort this child. Do this at least once a day for the next two weeks. After that, take a look at how you are feeling. Connect with your feelings by asking yourself: "How do I feel about this situation now?"

If you are still feeling deep bouts of shame, you may want to consider talking to someone. Sometimes, we have to go to a deeper level to get connected. You can do this more effectively by engaging with someone else who is listening objectively.

List your good qualities. By making this list, you can compare it to the list of defects. Put your defects and qualities side by side and ask yourself "Are these defects real?" If you write down the exaggeration, "Nobody likes me," cross it out and write the truth: "There are many who like me, and some don't."

Everyone has defective character traits, but they also have positive traits. Now, next to each defect, write a positive trait. Be as honest with yourself as you can. Spend at least twenty minutes on this.

Join a support group of positive-minded people. Getting involved with people you can share with is a great way to heal the pain of the past. Connect with people through a mastermind group online or in your local community.

You will find nowadays that connecting online with a group of people who share similar interests and goals boosts confidence and makes you feel a part of something. Get connected with others.

Years ago, when I started doing this, it changed my life. I was no longer "alone" but had found people with whom I could share my thoughts, feelings, and fears. Start to make a list of groups you could join. And this could be anything that is related to your hobbies, interests, or, if you want to go deeper, a group or person who specializes in therapy discussion.

Chapter Recap

We all have at least one primary pain point we deal with throughout life. Depending on the nature of the experience or condition that pain point will be connected to a favored escape strategy to numb or cope with the feelings you want to bury.

Shame is a powerful pain point that causes emotional scarring. To cope with this shame, we resort to behaviors that hurt either ourselves or others.

You can heal your shame by taking steps:

- Revisit your shame-based childhood.
- List your best qualities [and reframe those perceived as negative].
- Join a support group of positive-minded people.

Shame takes time to heal. Take positive action in moderation. Reach out to people you trust and talk about your situation. Do not expect instant results. Focus on building your awareness one day at a time. Your feelings of inadequacy and inferiority will become greatly diminished in the months and years to come.

In the next chapter I will get into the escape tactics and coping mechanisms used to cope with feelings of inadequacy, rejection, and deep-seated beliefs of inferiority. You will then learn the key strategies to recover from this.

"I hated every minute of training, but I said, 'Don't quit. Suffer now and live the rest of your life as a champion."

— **Muhammad Ali**

Chapter 10

Escape Tactics and Coping Mechanisms

"We all learn lessons in life. Some stick, some don't. I have always learned more from rejection and failure than from acceptance and success."

— **Henry Rollins**

Escape is used as a means to run away from the feelings of worthlessness. An addiction is an escape pattern used to numb and hide feelings of inferiority. As we will see, it disguises the problem, but fails to resolve it.

There are several ways of using avoidance tactics to cope with difficult moments in life. Let's take a look at these escape strategies and coping mechanisms, and the solutions we can implement to replace them.

Default Tactics: How We Learn to Cope

One pattern of dealing with our painful emotions is to flee from the point of origin causing the pain. When confronted with a situation that triggers fear, vulnerability, or those: "I'm less than," feelings, we take a "flight" action that removes us from experiencing the pain of rejection.

These are what we can call default tactics: We immediately revert to a strategy (coping mechanism) whose purpose is to protect the "ego" and the "self" from the pain point that has been triggered. There are many coping strategies that do this, as we can see from the upcoming list I have included. By default, the reaction we take to a stressful situation is a learned pattern. It is created from years of conditioning ourselves to run.

There is not much thought put into the coping mechanism, because once a reward is linked to the behavior, surrendering to a coping strategy becomes the normal route to take. From an observer's perspective this may appear as "out of control" behavior, but to the person bent on escaping it is the only way out.

Only it is not. We have just trained ourselves to believe so. But like any bad habit, we can recover. We can push reset and set ourselves up with different strategies that work. We are trapped only if we choose to be. That is to say, every time we are faced with a situation where we could be rejected, criticized or ostracized, fear kicks in. Driven by an emotion to survive, this leads to the mind seeking some form of relief.

Now, we know logically that the best way through any problem or adversity is to tackle the problem head on. By overcoming adversity we grow stronger. When we flee through addictive coping practices we are not dealing with the situation.

By avoiding rejection, we just stay fearful of more rejection in the future. By escaping from a social situation because we feel inferior, we just stay inferior. Nothing changes. By learning to reset your habits and coping mechanisms, you will learn to react and take action in a healthy way.

Now, think about a pain point that you have: Are you dealing with difficult relationships? Is there a problem at work? Do you struggle to carry on a conversation in a social situation? Is the fear of criticism so painful that you feel helpless? Is there someone in your life that makes you feel inferior or worthless?

When a pain point is triggered, an escape route or coping strategy is chosen. It becomes your method for survival. You come to depend on it more than anything else. This is the start of how people develop addictions and self-defeating behaviors. They start feeding into a habit to avoid or escape from the pain of dealing with a painful reality. This could be through drugs, alcohol, gambling, sex, or even endless hours of television.

While you are escaping from your pain, what seemingly brings you relief now has a heavy price to pay later. By choosing to numb out these feelings you are setting yourself up for failure later on.

Most people have developed at least one primary escape technique in their life, and many more people have multiple coping strategies depending on the situation they need to flee from. One escape strategy functions as the primary method to cope, but may include other methods of escape as well.

Avoidance Tactics and Coping Strategies

There are many ways people cope with their feelings of inadequacy, rejection, and deep-seated beliefs of inferiority. Part of the cycle of dealing with your uncomfortable emotions is to apply a coping strategy that delivers a specific outcome.

This could be an end result meant to numb out your current reality so that you don't have to relive the pain you went through. If the escape strategy is successful (based on your conclusion) then it becomes your primary method of escape. In other words, you personalize your behavior, even if it delivers an outcome that damages your chances of success in other areas of your life.

The final conclusion is that you stay stuck, but you would rather stay there than experience rejection. One of the core coping strategies in this case is excuse-making, when we convince ourselves that "this is where I belong" because nobody else will accept me. Again, the cycle justifies the situation even when you have a strong desire to do something about it.

People have their favorites for handling those tough feelings of social isolation, fear of being rejected, and not measuring up. You may feed into one or more of these behaviors. Later, we will go over the cycle and how you can minimize and disengage these behaviors. But for now, realize that everyone has at least one of the following coping strategies that act as their primary strategy.

Here is a list that makes up the bulk of the escape and avoidance tactics. Do you recognize any of these coping strategies from the list below?

- Isolating

- Counterattacking (defensiveness)

- Addictive behaviors and numbing the pain
- Blaming
- Criticizing others
- Denial
- Failing to take responsibility
- Avoiding meeting new people
- Avoiding responsibility
- Getting angry (tantrums)
- Being passive
- Sabotaging self/others
- Excessive worrying
- Labeling
- Complaining
- Comparisons
- Holding onto resentments
- Thinking negatively about someone
- Being obsessive about something
- Rationalizing
- Feeling the fear and doing nothing about it.
- Focusing on the past

If you see anything here that resembles your coping strategy, make a note of it so that you can come back to it later when we go over some strategies for dealing with this.

Here are five core areas you could be using escape as a means to cope.

1. Addiction

The first choice for many people is to cope through using an addiction of some sort, and, these days, there are enough addictions to fulfill anyone's needs. Your choice of addiction depends on what works best for you, but the usual contenders are: alcohol, drugs, smoking, or sex. Addictions are tough to break, but there is great freedom on the other side if you break through.

Just to make a note, it is beyond the scope of this book to get into addiction recovery. If you are addicted to any substance or process, I suggest you get professional help. Just keep in mind that addictions could have a direct relation to how you try to escape from painful situations.

The addiction masks the problem, and in itself, is not the core problem. It is merely a symptom of the underlying issues that have not been dealt with.

Action Steps

Is there an addiction that serves as your primary coping mechanism? If so, what is it? If this is something you want to stop doing because it is destructive, then seek out professional help if you have to.

Depending on the seriousness of this, it may be worth it just to talk to someone before making any decisions. If addiction is your core coping strategy, taking action toward eliminating it would make a huge difference in your quality of life.

2. Impressing People and Showing Off (Disproving Your Unworthiness)

Rejection mindset has its power in gaining approval from others. We do this by seeking praise or encouragement without giving any back. We want to be recognized to remove the pain of feeling invisible. We all want to be accepted in some way.

Impressing other people has its origins in childhood. It could be that as a child or young adult, our achievements, no matter how small, were rarely recognized. We were ignored. Our efforts were not validated unless we did something that was extraordinary such as making the dean's list at school or excelling at sports.

This can be a big one for many people, and if impressing others is one of our strategies, observing and replacing this faulty technique is a huge step.

Some ways that we might try to impress people are:

1. Telling everyone about your achievements before they even ask. This usually comes across as a desperate call for attention.

2. Making your achievements or efforts seem superior to another person's. This could also involve sabotaging another person's work or efforts to gain notoriety over your own. It is extreme, but it happens.

3. Seeking approval from others to validate our worth (look what I did, aren't you impressed?).

4. Overemphasizing or exaggerating your success and achievements. Desperate for gaining recognition, we exaggerate what we have accomplished, hoping to impress others. Here is a secret. Most people aren't impressed and don't care.

Action Steps

In what ways do you try to impress people? How could you counteract this? Here is what you can do: Write down and identify the reasons why you feel the need to impress people. What emotions are you going through at the time? Are you feeling inferior to the other person? You want them to like you? You want to be accepted as an equal?

Take time to think on this. For example, you may have an issue with feeling like a failure. Therefore, you try to impress people who are successful. Work through each of the situations when you do this. Map out the conclusions you come to. The next time you are in a situation when the pain point of inferiority or defectiveness is triggered, you can recognize it and stop it before it kicks into action.

3. Going on the Defensive (Counterattacking)

Overly sensitive people tend to get defensive when they feel attacked or criticized. In many cases, what is mistaken as an attack on character could simply be prodding for fun or someone making an innocent joke. But because of our hypersensitivity we fail to see it as any other way.

In other situations, it could be an evaluation at work or being unjustly blamed for something. Whatever the case, the reaction is to take a stand and counterattack. But this can have more damage than good.

People who fight back tend to lash out at times without provocation. They may think that they just had to do it when, in fact, the other person meant no real harm.

Action Steps

Look for ways that you take a counterattack stance. Are you always ready to fight back? Do you look for opportunity to show them who's who and what's what? Do you always feel bad after lashing out?

Watch for those situations when you are ready to attack. This comes when you are expecting something to be done against you, or you are ready to defend your position at all costs, even if you are wrong. Now, what can you do instead of counterattacking?

Here are a few steps to take:

Observe carefully the situations when you are critical of others. Is it when you feel devalued? Unappreciated? Is your shame (pain point) triggered? Do you feel inferior to someone you just met because they are smarter, richer, or more intelligent?

We counterattack as a way to overcompensate. When our feelings of defectiveness are triggered, counter attacking is the coping strategy that is kicked into action.

Make a note of when you counterattack and for what reason. For example, feelings of worthlessness could be a key pain point for you. If it is, when this is triggered, your response is to make up for your worthlessness by choosing a coping strategy such as counter attacking, blaming, or attempting to impress people.

By observing and catching yourself as it is happening, you can choose to end the behavior right away. In most cases we just respond by instinct. But once you see yourself acting out, you can intervene on yourself and put an end to it.

4. Escaping Responsibility

Avoiding situations where you are responsible for other people could be a major area you are sensitive about. This could be a situation at work or at home. A parent could avoid interacting with their spouse or children. At work, you could avoid responsibility or challenges that involve risk. That risk includes the fear of failing at a project or fear of failing to live up to expectations.

When filled with uncertainty and self-doubt, the natural instinct is to flee or hide. By escaping responsibility, we can avoid the stress and anxiety that goes with it.

Action Steps

Are there situations in which you flee from responsibility? For example, taking care of someone, a project at work, or owning up to a mistake. Take notice of the areas of your life that you definitely don't want to be held accountable for.

Then, hold yourself *accountable*. Tell yourself that there is nobody who can do this except you. Push yourself to see the actions through to the end. Do this several times and it will get easier.

5. Self-Sabotage

You struggle to accept yourself as you are. So when you have a little success and things start to go well, you look for ways to derail your success. Self-sabotage is practiced through several methods or tactics.

You could indulge in binge eating, drinking, or overspending to destroy the little good things. If you get a new job that is challenging or there is risk that you could fail, you could sabotage it by showing up late at work or disregarding company policy to get yourself fired.

You want to escape the expectations placed on you to avoid failing before it happens. You do not want any kind of recognition because, deep down, you feel that you don't deserve it.

You commit destructive acts that cause others to ignore you or take you out of the loop. They may say that you are unreliable or cannot be trusted. But just the opposite is true.

Deep down, you want to be recognized, but you cannot allow yourself to be in a position that attracts attention. This is also a way to avoid forming relationships with people. If they get close to you then your cover is blown.

Five Ways You Sabotage Yourself

1. If you are successful in losing weight, you could suddenly go on a binge and gain more weight than you had before.

2. In a new relationship that is going well, you have an affair or start to avoid the person you are dating.

3. At work, you show up late or create conflict in the office to get terminated.

4. If you are showing signs of progress in a recovery program, you could slip back into old behaviors and ruin your recovery.

5. If you are successful at saving some money, you suddenly splurge and spend the money you saved…and then some!

The goal with self-sabotage is to keep you stuck in your "comfort zone." This is related to the cycle we looked at earlier. When you struggle with feelings of unworthiness or the defeatist belief that you are no good, your natural inclination will be to ruin your success through actions that defeat you.

Action Steps

1. Think of a time that you experienced feelings of inferiority or rejection. Now, what is the escape method you used to deal with this? Was this effective? What were the advantages to escaping?

2. Think of an alternative action you could take that would replace your escape tactics. For example, instead of watching TV excessively to relax, you can read for 20-30 minutes or do something creative.

3. In what ways do you justify and give power to your escape strategies? Is it to relieve stress or to help you get through a difficult time? Make a list of the excuses you use that gives power to your escape plan.

Chapter Recap

Escape strategies have only one goal in common: to isolate us from the pain point. A situation that threatens to expose our defects is the perfect opportunity. We all have our own favorite form of escape.

This could be wrapped up in procrastination techniques or self-destructive behaviors such as excessive drug or alcohol abuse. The goal is to avoid pain and escape reality. We pick up these learned techniques from experience and experimentation.

When we find something that works, meaning it relieves our stress or helps to release anxiety, we adopt it as a strategy that works. This becomes our default practice. The more we do it, the more natural it becomes.

Now, let's keep moving on because in the next chapter we are covering *The Breakthrough Cycle* that will give you a big advantage to conquering your rejectionist mindset.

Chapter 11

Guilt-Free Responsibility

"You must take personal responsibility. You cannot change the circumstances, the seasons, or the wind, but you can change yourself. This is something you have charge of."

— **Jim Rohn**

The reason many people struggle to move forward is that they insist on holding onto their resentments and pain years after the fact. After being criticized, rejected, or mistreated in some way, they want some form of apology from the people who are responsible.

These people who hold onto their grudges are the only ones who can help themselves. They wait for the day when someone else finally gives them the love they deserve which leads to being disappointed all over again.

Meanwhile, their lives grow shorter and their condition does not change; they stay stuck in a rut, blaming and lashing out at others. They are content to blame and point the finger at the people who failed them, and their lives will be filled with resentment, anxiety, and depression.

But you are not like most people. You want it to change, right? Then here is what you have to do:

Stepping It Up

Taking full responsibility for your life and your current emotional state [happy or unhappy] is how we take charge of our lives. By stepping up and putting an end to blaming and finger pointing, you can take control of your own destiny.

You should never put the future of your own happiness in the hands of anyone else other than yourself. When you fully take responsibility for your own emotional well-being you stop putting that responsibility onto other people.

This puts you in a position of empowerment. While spending time with people we like is critical to our well-being, trusting in someone to balance our lives and take care of us could lead to disappointment down the road.

Making a decision to stop blaming others for your unhappiness is taking a healthy approach to being responsible for what happens in your own life. This does not mean you have to forget what happened in the past, but you do have to move on from it. This can only happen when you choose to live life on your terms by making a firm decision and following through with action to create a positive and fulfilling future.

When you wait for someone else to step up and take charge, you lose the chance to make the situation better. You miss out on the opportunity to heal yourself. You give up the moment to take yourself to the next level. Do not wait for someone else to take responsibility for your life.

Here are five ways you can start to practice intentional responsibility in your life:

1. Make a Decision to Act Responsibly

The one factor that makes all the difference is your willingness and courage to accept yourself as you are, defects and all, so you can move on with your life. The moment you decide to take responsibility, that's when a major shift takes place.

But what do I mean by taking responsibility? You are already responsible for many things: your family, getting to work on time, or community events. In fact, people who have an inferiority complex excel at being responsible because they want to please people more than the average person. But that is not the kind of responsibility I am talking about. You need to be responsible to yourself. You owe it to yourself, because nobody else is going to give it to you.

As bestselling author and motivational speaker Brian Tracy said: *"Real responsibility is realizing that nobody is coming to the rescue."*

This means that you have to stop waiting around for someone else to fix your problems. If this is a problem for you, keep this in mind: Expecting others to carry you is another form of self-defeat.

You will not learn to heal when you place unreasonable demands on people. And by unreasonable demands, I mean expecting others to carry your burden, your troubles, and your grievances. Nobody can lift that much and you don't have a right to ask anyone to do so.

2. Own Your Behavior

By taking full responsibility and owning your behavior you gain tremendous power over your emotional state. When you say things like, "I wish he wouldn't make me feel that way," or "She should treat me better than that," you are passing that responsibility onto the other person. You lose power this way.

Having expectations to be liked or treated well all the time are unrealistic. And nobody can make you feel a certain way regardless of how he or she treats you. You take care of the way you react and that is it.

If you react in a defensives manner and lash out you will lose control of your emotions. You will resort to your old behavior of blaming and criticizing. This leads to taking on the victim role. Then the downward spiral begins again, and you have fallen into the defeatist cycle once more.

Own your behavior by observing how you respond. This is a habit you can implement right now. By getting focused and making yourself aware of how you are feeling, how you want to feel, and how you will react when someone is acting in a manner that is unacceptable, you gain greater control over your emotions. Instead of being at the mercy of someone else's response or emotional turmoil, you get to choose how you are feeling today.

3. "It's Them, Not Me." Disowning Your Behavior

When it comes to being rejected, the fear can only originate from one location: Within you. Rationalizing that it comes from others is a lie.

You create the feeling and the fear of being rejected in relationships, social situations, and within your work environment.

It is true that others may "put you down," but this only works with your permission. Nobody can reject you, or at least they cannot project the emotion onto you. Sure, you may be turned down for a job, ignored in public or social settings, or told to "get lost" by a member of the opposite sex, but how you take it is your choice.

People who fear rejection are reacting from an old pattern that exists. If you set aside the fear and decide that it is not going to control your emotions, the situation will not bother you in the least.

As long as you think the external world has power over you and can manipulate you into reacting in a certain way or feeling a certain way, and depending on how you are treated, emotions are going to be influenced by other situations and people at all times.

You can change this today if you decide to. Choose to take responsibility for your emotional state. When you feel the fear of rejection coming on, or you start to experience the trigger that puts you in that mindset, realize that it is up to you how to react. Will you give in to your feelings of inferiority? Or will you talk back and stand up against those negative emotions? You have a choice in your response to everything.

Tell yourself: "I am responsible for my own state. Nobody else is responsible. Only me."

4. Dealing with Blame and Forgiveness

Holding onto blame is a primary coping mechanism. It makes a victim out of us. We spend a part of our lives wanting an apology. By projecting blame onto the people responsible for injury, we keep the hurt alive. It never heals.

I have found only one solution that works best for this: Practice forgiving the people you blame. Visualize yourself having a conversation with the person. Tell them you now understand that, because they were going through their own pain and did not have the skills to deal with it, they projected it onto you. It is up to you if you want to hold onto it or let it go. By letting it go and replacing it with a "gentle understanding," you set both yourself and the other person free.

This could be harder for some people than others, especially if it involved mental or physical abuse. That makes a much deeper cut, and they may need a professional to talk with. Do what has to be done, but take action right now. Do not wait. You can start with a visualization technique or having a "mirror" discussion and then follow up with any further counseling if needed.

Forgiveness takes effort, and if you cannot forgive the other person at this stage of your life, then that is okay. You can work on forgiving yourself for carrying the burden all these years. Forgive yourself for all the self-criticism or self-sabotage you have caused.

If others were exposed to your negative behaviors or you made them suffer somehow, you can forgive yourself for this too. Make forgiveness a habit and a way of living. By doing this, you set yourself and others free. By not doing it you remain in a state of victimization. Which would you rather do?

5. Make Responsibility an Active Choice

It takes courage to take control of your life. Too many people are caught up in all the hang-ups and resort to petty actions of blaming, criticisms, and holding onto old beliefs that continue feeding into negative behaviors.

In order to reset your old ways, you have to make responsibility a conscious choice. It rarely happens by default. I have found that the mindfulness habit really works in this situation. When we make ourselves purposefully aware of the objectives we are reaching for, through the mindfulness approach, you can add a boost to your responsibility.

For example, choosing to be inferior to others is a choice. Nobody can make you feel this way. Your choices define you, and if you choose to be rejected then you will be. You develop a rejectionist persona where, when you actually feel like a reject, you create more of it in your daily life. If you turn around and say, "That's it; I've had enough. I will not let this situation or person defeat me!" that is the ultimate choice.

Watch for situations that you are trying to avoid taking responsibility. You can see this happening when you criticize, blame, condemn, or talk negatively about someone or a situation.

Denying your responsibility is pushing it away onto others. This is not to say you have to take the blame for everything that happens, but before seeking blame, seek solutions. People who live in fear of being condemned or judged may resort to finger pointing or worse.

You can turn this around by observing your interactions with people. Even reflecting on past moments that happened just today and yesterday, and seeing where you acted with selfishness or tried to escape, can have a big impact on your positive mindset.

Chapter Recap

Be aware of situations that you are blaming, condemning, criticizing, or passing off responsibility to others.

Your actions are your own. Your thoughts and feelings are your own. Make a conscious effort to be aware of what and how you are thinking, feeling and responding.

Owning responsibility for your actions and reactions is the surest way to preventing resentment. Taking full responsibility for your life and your current emotional state [happy or unhappy] is how we take charge of our lives.

By stepping up and putting an end to blaming and finger pointing, you can take control of your own destiny.

The **5 strategies** discussed are:

1. Make a Decision to Act Responsibly

2. Own Your Behavior

3. "It's Them, Not Me." Disowning Your Behavior

4. Blaming and Practice Forgiveness

5. Make Responsibility an Active Choice

Chapter 12

Break-Free Strategies for Living Rejection Free

"Your self-confidence is directly connected to how much you feel you are making a difference in the world."

— Brian Tracy

In this chapter, I am going to present eight strategies that you can implement to create a foundation for building confidence, empowering your self-esteem, and to provide you with the techniques to help push your growth beyond your current limitations.

I recommended that you start right away by taking action and pushing yourself to break free of the "mental chains" of rejection. This means working to eliminate all excuses for feeling crappy about who you are.

We are focusing on getting rid of the rejected victim and building a new persona, the YOU that is free, confident, and filled with a new form of energy. It is time to RESET the way you have been thinking and feeling. The one way to achieve this is through taking specific, intentional action. If you wanted to gain immediate control of your life, this is where we will start.

Break-Free Strategies

Each exercise presented here is simple enough you can implement into your daily routine. It just takes some organization so that you are ready to tap into your mindfulness and know what to do when the situation calls for it.

Let's dive into the strategies:

Strategy #1: Apply the Substitution Technique for Creating Lasting Change

Throughout this book we have discussed several key strategies for changing behavior, discarding old beliefs, and forming a positive mindset to heal our rejectionistic beliefs.

In order to facilitate rapid changes, we can practice the **substitution technique** to further reinforce these changes.

The substitution technique, or replacement technique as it is sometimes called, can solve many problems for us when it comes to working change into our lives. You can find opportunity everyday to use it and, if applied consistently, will help you to develop your relationships, become a better communicator, as well as do things differently to generate better results.

It acts as a major game changer when it comes to healing bad habits and overcoming root negativity. The challenge is in developing the awareness of when you need to use it.

Let's take an example: If you are in the habit of talking down to yourself, let's turn it around using this replacement technique. Instead of talking negatively to yourself with "I suck at this," you could say, "I am now learning how to do this better."

The idea is to reinforce your thoughts with positivity. In the case of feeling rejected, when confronted with a situation when someone says "No", instead of telling yourself, "Well, I've been shot down again", turn the situation around.

Begin by replacing the negative thoughts you have with empowering thoughts. Substitute your first default belief that you're no good with a belief that empowers you. Do not accept any thought that builds on your doubt and fear. Instead of "I am no good" you say, "I am awesome"; "My life sucks" is substituted with "I am so lucky to have everything that I do." And then, you can validate this by referring to the gratitude list you made earlier.

To recap, use the **substitution technique** for replacing:

- harmful, negative words with positive expressions. You can include affirmations that work amazingly well when it comes to forming a positive mindset.

- worry-based, fearful thinking with positive images that encourage immediate action. This will move you closer toward your objectives.

- destructive bad habits with good habits that leads to positive results while creating a better process for doing things.

Use the Substitution Technique for Actions

When you catch yourself criticizing either yourself or others, you can replace this behavior with the opposite action. Instead of criticizing and judging, speak well of others. Build up their reputation. Stop yourself immediately and change this behavior from condemning and verbal criticism to praising the reputation of others.

Challenge yourself to do this for one week. Make it a conscious habit to convert all negative actions, behavior, and conversation into a stream of positive conviction.

Tell yourself "I am awesome!"

Tell others "You are great! I am so happy to have you in my life!"

This technique is a major game changer. Using this alone can have a major impact on how you live your life. Start using it right now!

Strategy #2: Identify Your Positive Characteristics

If someone asked you to list twenty things about yourself that you dislike, I bet you could do it easily. It is always easier to take the way you are used to, such as beating yourself up emotionally or self-criticizing. Let's put an end to this, shall we?

I want you to make a list of ten things you like about yourself. This can be anything you want, as long as it is a positive trait. Then, you will tell yourself why each is a positive trait.

Here is a list I made up so you can see how easy it is:

- I wake up every morning early to get the kids ready for school. This is a good trait because it shows that I am a good parent.

- I hold the door open for people when they are behind me. This is a positive trait because it shows that I am considerate of others.

- I read for twenty minutes every evening. This is a positive trait because it shows that I am trying to broaden my knowledge.

- I wake up early and do ten minutes of exercise. This is a positive trait because it shows I am serious about my health and fitness.

- I help my children with their homework. This is a positive trait because it shows I am intelligent and have patience.

- I am a good friend to the people who know me. This is a positive trait because it shows loyalty and trustworthiness.

Even if you can only think of one or two things right now, that is enough to get started. You can build up your "like list" over the course of the next few days or weeks.

What matters most at this point is you get something down on paper and make it obvious to yourself that you are not all bad. In fact, the more good stuff you discover about yourself, the harder it will be for you to find any excuse to feel inadequate or rejected.

Strategy #3: Give Away As Much Love As You Can…and Start Doing It Now

I knew a man once who, in the final days of his life, said that he had only one regret: He wished that he had loved people more and had given more of himself to the world. He died believing that he had not fulfilled his life's mission because he held back too much. This man said that he had always feared being rejected, and so to not put himself in that situation, he remained isolated and distant.

When you have a situation where you feel rejected by the people who are supposed to love you the most, there is a natural tendency to hold back on giving anything. Afraid of opening yourself up to vulnerability, you keep to yourself. Emotions are clamped tight and little is shared. You have a desire to reach out and be yourself, and to connect with people around you, but, uncertain of the risk involved, you withdraw and connect with nobody.

Introverts are infamous for this, but you do not have to be an introvert to hold back love. It takes great fear to hold onto love, and even more courage to give it away. You think it is courageous to hold onto your love until you find someone who is worthy of taking it, but the opposite is true.

We have to let go of what we are afraid of. For those of us with social fears, holding on tightly is a coping mechanism. But letting go of that fear is the path to healing what we have been afraid of this entire time. Letting go is the pathway to making it all okay.

Gradually let yourself go by giving and opening up pieces of yourself a bit at a time. This could be a kind gesture, a kind word, or a smile to a stranger. I know these seem like simple actions, but as trivial as they may appear, doing this once a day is going to have a major impact on your self-confidence and have a dramatic shift in the way you feel.

Start offering to help people more. Give away what you have been hiding. You are not taking anything with you, so what are you waiting for? I know the fear involved in this. There is the old pain point of vulnerability and being open to injury. Well, if you wait for the perfect moment, you will lose all the moments.

Your social rejectionist persona will not stand a chance against this. I still struggle with this, but those days and weeks when I stop caring about looking silly are the best days for me. On days when I hold on with fear, allowing nobody to get close, it feels like I am putting a clamp around my heart. Do not do this if you want to recover.

By reaching out, you will attract more friendships and you will attract more business as well. People love to do business with those who are open and honest. Let people know what you are all about, and soon, you will be busier than you ever hoped possible.

Action Step #1

Today you have to reach out to one person and say something that you would normally resist saying. This could be as simple as saying "Hi" or letting someone know that you appreciate them. Expressing gratitude is an action.

Action Step #2

Build on your social relationships this week. Make a goal with yourself to connect with five new people a week. Even if it is just a brief introduction, start to put yourself out there. When I first did this, I realized how terrified I was of the world. I have always been very closed-minded emotionally with people in my day-to-day activities.

When it was suggested that I connect with people just by having some simple communication, I started to get to know people. I was no longer trying to impress them, but they were interested in who I was and what I was doing. When I took an interest in them, most people reciprocated. So start to expand on your relationships.

Here is what you can do:

- Organize a get-together party and invite people you do not know.
- Create an online friendship group and connect with people through Facebook or other social media.
- Get interested in other people and what they are doing, what their dreams and aspirations are, and always offer to help if there is anything they need.

Strategy #4: Accept the Things You Cannot Change

There is a saying in Alcoholics Anonymous: "God, grant me the serenity to accept the things I cannot change, the courage to change the things I can, and the wisdom to know the difference."

One of the reasons people stay stuck is the resistance to accepting the things that happened, the events that can't be changed. At a deeper level, they wish that they had been treated better or that things had been different somehow.

Not accepting what happened freezes the event that never changes. Wishing things had been different and wanting to do something about it, we realize that there is no way out. So, we resort to a coping strategy that consumes our life. In other words, we refuse to accept the things we cannot change.

When we can move beyond it, with the courage to "accept the things we cannot change," we empower ourselves to move forward. The wisdom is in knowing and recognizing what can be changed and what can't. Past events cannot be changed. Yes, we know this, but knowing it and believing it are two different things.

We may have spent a lifetime holding onto what was done, but not accepting it. And it isn't easy to accept the mistakes and failures in our past. Things were done and we were injured. We want an apology or someone to own up to his or her behavior that caused us emotional suffering. Whatever it may be, it is time to take responsibility. The past doesn't owe us anything; we owe it to ourselves to start acting differently today.

Years ago, I had to accept that the emotional pain I was holding onto was real and that only I could change it. Only I could unleash the courage to move on. Nobody was going to fix me or take care of my wounded child. I had two choices: move on or stay where I was. Courage is feeling the fear and doing it anyways.

Take a situation that happened and write out what happened. How do you wish it had turned out? What would you do if you could change it?

Make a short list of action steps to move you forward. Have the courage to take that first step. Recite the prayer above and remember it by heart. When you find yourself going back wishing that something had never happened, remind yourself that it is unchangeable. It always was.

But today, you have the courage to make anything happen. So, ask for the serenity to accept what you can't change. This doesn't mean that you have to accept it, just that you need the serenity to do so, or the willingness.

Then, decide what you can change. Is it your attitude toward the situation? A Destructive habit that's keeping you stuck? Work through this, and you will see that you have all the power and strength you need to get through anything. You are only as weak as you believe yourself to be. Look up to yourself, forgive, and focus on your steps taking you forward and not back.

Strategy #5: The Seven-Day Anti-Criticism Challenge

Criticism is a destructive form of negativity. Delivered in the wrong pitch or manner, it can destroy someone's confidence and leave them emotionally "crippled" for life. If you grew up in a very critical environment, and so you know the damage that this can cause. This is why I want you to try the "**Seven-Day Anti-Criticism Challenge!**"

Make a challenge with yourself that you are not going to criticize or say anything negative about anyone no matter what they do. This does not mean you have to be passive and just accept everything they do; rather, seek another way to express your feelings that is not along the lines of criticism or a sharp comeback.

Several months ago I challenged myself to do this. Within the first few days, I did not make it past a few hours without making a comment, opinion, or criticizing someone for something. In fact, I actually looked for defects in others and then exposed them.

Years of this conditioning led to the bad habit of complaining and a deep sadness I was living with after realizing how critical I actually was. No wonder I was always so miserable!

To combat this, I set up the anti-complaining strategy. It works like this: You have to make a pact with yourself that you will not say anything that damages another person's reputation. This includes everything from backstabbing to sarcastic remarks aimed at tearing down another person's reputation.

This form of negative attacking is extremely damaging, not to the person you are doing it to but to yourself. It is a form of hidden self-sabotage. It is so habitual that you are not even aware you are doing it.

For me, it was normal. So, I started the challenge. It took about two weeks before I could finally get through a full day without criticizing. It was not easy, but this is good. It showed how powerful the addiction was.

Once I stopped, everything changed — My perspective, my mood, and my desire to be right. It also eliminated my need to counterattack, which was one of my core negative coping strategies.

Action Steps

For the next seven days you are going to make a promise to yourself not to criticize or condemn yourself or others in any way. This will require a great amount of self-discipline. And you will likely fail many times. But that is okay. The goal is to eliminate your need to criticize yourself or others.

One of the most damaging practices that kills confidence is your own critical monster. You are going to kill that monster. You can even give it a name such as Whiner, Grouse, or Grump. Start from first thing in the morning and focus on your thoughts. Watch the people and situations that cause you to lash out or feel negative energy.

Buy a calendar and mark off every day that you went without having a critical thought about yourself or another person. By being critical of others you are, in fact, damaging your own self-esteem. By marking it down on a calendar, you can see the progress you are making. Turn this habit around into a positive one, and, when someone makes you angry or criticizes you, go ahead and think something good about that person.

When I started to do this, I felt totally different after I made it to day three. I had no idea how negative I was, not only toward myself but, toward others as well. It is a life-changing technique that drives your confidence up, and continues driving you forward to make solid improvements toward character by eliminating other defects.

Strategy #6: The "Two-Way Mirror Technique"

This is a great technique for calming anxiety and lowering your nervousness so that you can function and be yourself with others. Spend a few minutes with yourself in front of a mirror. It may feel uncomfortable at first, but after a few times, it will become a habit. Do this for just a few minutes in the morning. To save time, do it while styling your hair, shaving, putting on makeup, or brushing your teeth.

Talk positively to yourself. Do not criticize or condemn anything about yourself. Talk to yourself as if you were talking to a best friend. Be the best friend you have ever had. Give yourself positive advice.

Look yourself in the eye and just give yourself advice as if you would give it to someone you care about. Do this technique ten minutes a day first thing in the morning. It builds your confidence and centers your thoughts.

Here are some things you could say:

An achievement you recently had. Praise yourself and give credit for something you recently did. This does not have to be an over-the-top achievement. Just keep it simple.

Talk about the great day you are going to have. Pump yourself up by talking about all the great things you are going to do today. Will you spend time with friends, family, or your children? Will you do something fun that you have been looking forward to? The purpose of this is to get yourself into a positive frame of mind, and to develop a healthy mindset for the day.

Talk about someone you love and admire. This is a great way to start feeling good about people again. Talk to yourself about the most important people in your life.

Talk about someone you have resentment toward. Just as it is important to talk about the people you love, now talk about someone you have a difficult relationship with. Think of one good thing you can say about this person. Imagine he or she is staring back at you as you are having a conversation. This strategy removes the negative energy that builds up when you have to deal with difficult people.

Strategy #7: List the Evidence That Supports You as Defective

When you feel rejected by people or inferior to them somehow, you look for ways to validate the experience. The "victim" in you needs proof that you are not worthy of love, friendship, or attention. This is easy to do. The proof is everywhere if you want to find it.

What you are going to do here is come up with a case against your rejectionism. Just like in court, you are building a case against your feelings of inferiority. You have spent a lot of years living "one down" from everyone and everything.

Now you have to cast aside those feelings of doubt and believe in yourself to rise up and out of the "emotional mud" that is keeping you down. Your goal is to disprove the lies that are keeping you trapped. Show yourself that you are not guilty of being defective.

Here is what you are going to do:

List the evidence that you are worthless or unlovable. Come up with five to ten situations or scenarios that support your belief that "Yes, I am no good."

For example, when I go to a party or social gathering, everyone ignores me. Now this could be a belief that you have, but it is the reality of what you think. Is it true? Are people ignoring you or are they just so preoccupied with themselves that they do not notice you? What evidence do you have that you are being ignored? If someone does ignore you, so what? Does that still prove you are a social reject, or just that they are in a foul mood or being a jerk?

Similar to the example above, write down a situation or event that makes you feel defective. Is it a relationship? Do you feel jealous about someone? Do you feel self-conscious around others because they are looking down at you or judging you?

Write out the situation. Now start to brainstorm to prove if any of this is real. Try to actually convince yourself that others are better than you. Then, work on disproving it. Ask questions like I did above. Do this for every situation you are challenged with when your inferior trap is triggered. Talk back and get angry. Don't just surrender and give in. This feeds into your inferiority and makes you buy into the lie.

Strategy #8: Practice Using Words of Power

Words have an incredible impact on your emotions and mindset. A negative word spoken in the heat of the moment can ruin someone's day, and a positive expression could make it. Using words that empower not only you but also the people around you is one of the best ways to tap into your confidence. Words can alter a negative mindset if practiced over and over again.

When someone is stuck in a negative frame of mind, it is because they have thoughts that are running in negative modes. I realized that when I started to watch what I was saying, most of my words and expressions were foul words, meant to criticize someone else, and derogatory statements to downplay bad behavior.

In other words, I was creating my own misery again and again. And, no amount of self-help material was going to help unless I learned to curb this habit. So I made up a list of positive words. I went online and found empowering quotes. I learned to speak differently and, when I did, I thought differently too.

These positive words became the new way that I spoke. My inferior mind could not hold up the power of a good word spoken. You cannot have negative and positive thoughts occupy the same space at the same time. When you are feeling positive and focusing on this, everything is positive, and you operate from a place of positive energy.

Action Steps

1. Catch yourself when you use negative or self-criticizing words

2. Call yourself out when you say something negative or derogatory about yourself or someone else. Don't let yourself get away with it. Make a note of it and, more importantly, note how you were feeling at that moment. Was it stress or anger? By identifying the situation or persons involved, this could be your trigger.

Chapter Recap

We covered a list of actionable strategies in this chapter:

1. Apply the Substitution Technique for Creating Change: Replace your negative thinking with thoughts that empower you. Use this technique for replacing your beliefs, habits or worrisome thinking.

2. Identify the Positive Characteristics You Like About Yourself.

3. Give Away as Much Love As You Can…and Start Doing It Now.

4. Accept the Things You Cannot Change.

5. Take the **Seven-Day Anti-Criticism Challenge**: Make a challenge with yourself that you are not going to criticize or complain about anyone or anything for 7 days.

6. Practice the "Two-Way Mirror Technique.

7. Practice Using Words of Power.

8. List the Evidence That Supports You as Defective.

Try to implement these strategies at every opportunity you get. They really work to help you break through barriers, build personal and social confidence and give you more "ammo" to combat negative behavior, beliefs and anxiety.

In the next chapter we are going to talk about building social confidence and forging better relationships with people. If you are shy or consider yourself socially "awkward", I'll show you four strategies you can implement to make more friends and secure good relationships with people.

Chapter 13

Building Social Confidence and Better Relationships

"We are constituted so that simple acts of kindness, such as giving to charity or expressing gratitude, have a positive effect on our long-term moods. The key to the happy life, it seems, is the good life: a life with sustained relationships, challenging work, and connections to community."

— Paul Bloom

Building your social confidence with people is the key to managing your fears, doubts, and feelings of inferiority that may creep up on you in conversation. The issues we have surrounding rejection play a powerful role in the way we interact with and handle ourselves in situations that require us to be confident, real, and vulnerable.

The quality of the relationships you create with people adds happiness and value to both your life and theirs. You do not want to miss out on this. That is why bonding with others should be the main goal we focus on to build social skills, and open up our pathway of communication and understanding.

In this chapter we will cover six social confidence strategies you can put into action to build better relationships and deal with rejection when it comes up. By integrating these principles into your relationships at home, with people you just met, or at work, you will soon be creating relationships that last and add true value to your life.

The Social Interaction Strategies

When we fear being rejected, ostracized, or criticized, we close off from the world. In order to protect ourselves against the truth that others may throw at us, we may choose not to engage and bury our true selves deep to avoid emotional injury.

But here is the truth: These fears we have that isolate us from our social connections are self-created. Nobody is making you more fearful than you are. Nobody is rejecting you but yourself. Self-rejection and that inner critic will be like a voice standing behind you shouting obscenities while you are trying to act normal.

Remember this: when we are too focused on the externals, we suffer to control what we cannot. This is why you have to change your thoughts, emotions, and attitude from the inside.

Social Confidence Strategy #1: Condemn Another; Condemn Yourself—Avoiding Harsh Judgments

Judging others openly or in private is a destructive way to kill the reputation of another person. When you judge another person based on their actions, morals, or values that are different from yours, it places them at the bottom of the social ladder for others to clamber over.

Of course, there are times when we are judged for our actions. But judgment could be turned into something better, such as constructive criticism. Rather than judge and blame, we could provide advice, or recommend a better course of action if someone is in the wrong.

Here is something to keep in mind. The judgment you lay on another will eventually come back on you. People who judge harshly, criticize without thinking the situation through, and condemn others through gossip, or bad rumors are setting themselves up for the same unfair trials.

Unless you are born into perfection, the condemnation you deliver eventually becomes your own. You end up eating what you dish out.

One more point to remember is that although some people may listen to your rants, complaints, and opinions of another person's actions, at the same time they are fearful that they will also be on the end of that stick someday. It may actually separate you from the people you are trying to garner attention from and isolate you in a place all your own without any companions at all.

Judging others, passing blame, labeling, and tearing down another person's reputation through harsh criticisms puts you one step away from receiving the same treatment.

Here is what you can do instead. If someone does cause emotional injury that triggers your defenses to want to "react" and take revenge, think things through first. Here are three suggestions:

Approach the Person Directly

Approach the situation objectively and gather solutions for what they could have done differently. Try to understand what they did and why they did it. In many cases we approach a situation logically, try to decipher why something was done, and then start to judge someone based on the limited facts.

Have you ever addressed an opinion or labeled somebody harshly only to realize that you were wrong? Did you have all the facts? Did you really understand that person's point of view? It happens most of the time. In fact, most people are hardly right in their criticism, even though they try to justify it.

Do Not Limit the Playing Field

If you judge harshly you limit the playing field to the amount of friends and variety of different relationships you can have. You close your circle to only those people that think like you, act like you, and accept you without forming opinions.

When this happens you effectively isolate yourself from anything foreign that poses a threat to your ego. This is not a recommended path to take if your goal is to forge healthy relationships. New relationships mean a greater chance for opportunity while expanding your friendships, both personal and in business.

It's about changes you want to make ... in others

You condemn someone based on your limited beliefs and then validate this through coming up with all the excuses as to why it is not acceptable. When you condemn another you are pointing the finger around at yourself.

If you judge someone for the way they speak or the fashion that is worn, could it be because you in some way, would like to be just like them or act in the same manner but you cannot? You actually envy what they can do so as a way to make yourself feel more secure you label them for being different.

When you become more accepting of others, you open up the closed doors of your mind. When you become more accepting of yourself you open up the closed doors of your heart.

Take a look around you at all the differences in people. Walk into a coffee shop, sit down, and observe people as they interact, convey dynamic personalities, and are being who they are meant to be. You do not have to form opinions, likes, or dislikes. Just let the moment happen. Train yourself to accept people as they are. Then turn your emotions inside and look at yourself.

Are you judgmental because of fear? Is there something you want to change within but you are afraid to do so? Do you stick with the flock that you feel comfortable with because they do not judge or condemn you?

Step outside of who you are and be the person that you dream of being. Start to do the actions that person would take. Make it a focused effort to change from within. Then you will see real growth take place.

Social Confidence Strategy #2: Assess the situation from the other Point Of View

One of the most critically damaging mistakes we make in our social relationships is failing to understand the emotions and thoughts of another person. People form opinions, have ideas, share their experiences openly, and in daily interactions, do things that seem completely bizarre or out of character.

It is called being human, and when we come to gain an understanding of the actions or words expressed by someone else, even if we are hurt by what they have done, it deepens our sense of empathy.

Empathy is what you need to see the viewpoint of others from their perspective, and not only your own.

Similarly in relationships with our children, spouses, friends and colleagues we encounter situations when the other person is, from our own perspective, wrong in their choice of actions, opinion or words. However, if we step into their shoes and broaden our angle of perception, we can gain a greater understanding of the situation and avoid making false accusations.

Switching POV Is the Key to Successful Social Connections

Henry Ford, one of the most successful businessmen in history, said: "If there is any one secret of success, it lies in the ability to get the other person's point of view and see things from that person's angle as well as from your own."

Similarly, if you have troubles with your spouse, it may be because you just need to put yourself in your spouse's shoes to understand what they are up to. If you have the ability to change your point of view, you can not only avoid a lot of troubles and hassles but you can also predict the next move, which will be helping you in living a successful life.

POV and Rejection

One of the factors that lead to a rejection is that we are only seeing the outcome from our angle. You start to talk to yourself in negative tones and say things like, "I was rejected because I'm no good," or "They must have seen right through me."

Could it be possible that that person is having a bad day? Could it be that you just are not what they needed at the moment? The rejection, as we learned earlier in this book, is not always about you. It is more about the other person in most cases. It is about emotions and circumstances that are largely beyond your control.

Once you move away from the victim role you can easily view the scene from another angle that gives you a broader scope of what is really happening.

Social Confidence Strategy #3: Treat Others as Equals

One of the biggest mistakes people make when trying to forge better relationships is to automatically think that they are somehow above others based on social status, wealth, or position. The truth is that when stripped of all titles and material possessions, everyone is playing on the same field. Some might be faster than others, and others are smarter; but the bottom line is that we all have our strengths and weaknesses.

Equality and Ego

Ego plays a very important part in this role. The ego wants to be better than anyone else. In fact, it does not need any evidence to prove this. It already believes it, and it wants you to believe it too. The ego puts itself above all else. It only cares about self-preservation and it will climb over anyone to put itself at the top of the chain.

Many people, who are put in positions of power, whether those positions are in politics, business, or family, automatically assume that because they have been handed a big title, it puts them above everyone else. The little people are beneath everything else. The ego is a corrupt entity and grasps at anything to justify its existence. Be aware of this and you can control it. Allow it to dominate you and it will.

When you treat people as equals, even if they have less than you do, remember that it is relevant. Just because they have less does not mean they are less. Just because your position or title is above theirs does not mean you are the captain and commander of wisdom.

In today's world the most effective organizations and families are those who train their people to think for themselves. Most people are accustomed to feeling less than they are. They were perhaps raised that way by their parents to be dependent, and so when something comes up, they want someone else higher up [daddy or the CEO] to fix it.

But in fact, most people I have come across, when given the challenge and treated as an equal and not a subordinate, are able to work it out themselves with just the right amount of support needed from friends or mentors. Let them grow up with the knowing that they are free to be who they want to be and that mommy and daddy will accept them no matter what. They are your equals in every way.

Instead of just pointing the finger and assigning blame or lashing out a punishment, take the time to figure out what is going on and what working together to make the situation better can do. You will discover that, by leveling the playing field, you will have more respect and admiration from those around you.

Social Confidence Strategy #4: Confront the Fear of Vulnerability in Relationships

Perhaps the greatest obstacle that prevents us from forging better relationships is the feeling of vulnerability that comes with connecting with others. We are afraid to trust that we will not get rejected or hurt. We put up fronts, act the part, but if someone tries to get to know the real you, the defenses go up and we retreat back into our holes of comfort and safety.

On a superficial level, most people "act" confident, in control, and are quite sure of themselves. Inside, they have fear and uncertainty, doubt, and a deeply hidden inferiority complex. To be afraid, to have low confidence, and to doubt yourself are all things that we fear, and so we try to cover them up with an inflated ego, boasting, or acting confident.

Look Fear in the Eye

Allowing yourself to be vulnerable can be an uncomfortable experience. You feel exposed and open to attack from criticism. You fear that someone may find out who you really are and expose the truth to the world, shattering the false self-image you worked so hard to build up.

The ego, your false self, is always on guard; it has its defenses up round the clock and will do anything to protect its self-interests. This "defense" appears as a friend in times of need; a protector that keeps you safe. It is, in fact, just the opposite.

In order for us to effectively make healthy and deep connections with others, you must concentrate to remove the fear of being vulnerable. Allow yourself to make mistakes. Let others see that you are willing to risk everything in order to be a better friend, spouse, or business partner.

By facing your fears of exposure and vulnerability, by lowering your defenses, you are not making yourself weaker but just the opposite. You are letting others in; you are giving them a chance to know the real you, and what this does is build a level of deep trust. And TRUST is one of the core foundational pillars for building solid relationships.

Chapter Recap

Focusing on building strong relationships is the foundation of overcoming social fears and rejection. The relationship begins with building trust with yourself. Then, you can have a more positive experience socializing and conversing with other people.

Here are the 4 strategies we looked at:

- Avoiding harsh judgments.
- Assess the situation from the other POV.
- Treat others as equals.
- Confront the Fear of vulnerability in relationships.

A few additional communication tactics I recommend are:

- Remember people's names, and address them by their name several times during the conversation.
- Listen and don't interrupt or try to give your opinion before hearing the entire story.
- Complement someone on a good idea when they share their thoughts with you.

Now, in the last chapter, I'll give you twelve effective habits that are going to change the way you think and feel. These habits are critical in helping you to keep making progress and avoid slipping back into old patterns of defeat.

Chapter 14

Twelve Habits to Reset Your Day

"How different our lives are when we really know what is deeply important to us, and keeping that picture in mind, we manage ourselves each day to be and to do what really matters most."

— **Stephen Covey,** bestselling author of
The 7 Habits of Highly Effective People

We have covered a lot of ground in this book up until now. We have looked at the cycle of rejection, how your rejectionism and an inferiority mindset have controlled your life, and the strategies you can put into action to recover from this.

I have shared with you the step-by-step actions for changing your beliefs. We also discussed the different ways people deal with fearful emotions through escape, and the trigger responses compelling us to act out.

Then, we looked at establishing a new, healthy cycle habit to replace the cycle of rejection and implement better strategies for building self-confidence. Now we know that recovery from rejection is a set of forward actions taken consistently.

By taking action, we can push ourselves further than we ever dreamed possible. By confronting the fears that are holding us back, we are now stronger and more resilient to do something about it.

In this last chapter, we will focus on action driven habits you can develop in order to avoid slipping back into old behaviors, fears, and habits. Even after taking action on the recovery steps I discussed earlier, it can be easy to slip back into our old patterns if we just stay where we are. Once we have made progress in our recovery, we should continue to work harder to keep moving forward.

If you are not taking care of your behaviors a little every day, you will find yourself slipping back into the old behaviors that could end up damaging your self-esteem and confidence.

When you let your emotions go unnoticed and negative feelings twist your thoughts, you can revert back to old habit patterns. I do not want that to happen to you. I want you to continue to grow, and to use this book as a guide to keep you moving forward in a positive direction.

Twelve Habits to Build Better Routines

Here are twelve daily habits that you can put into action right away. You can focus on just one habit at a time, or work on building several habits throughout the week.

Some of these habits may seem like common sense or simple. You don't have to adopt all of them. Pick the ones you think would benefit you the most and stick with it for thirty days. Once you hit the thirty days mark, make it a goal to strive for another thirty days. According to health psychology researcher Phillipa Lally it takes a *minimum of 66 days* to implement a new habit, and could take as many as 254 days depending on the person and circumstances.

If you skip a day in your new habit development, make sure you pick it up again the next day. If you let it go and continue to put it off, you will get out of the habit and have to start over. If you give up after a few weeks, do not beat yourself up over it.

What is important is that you try new things and keep attempting to direct your habits to work for you in a positive way. Building a new routine is encouraging and starts moving your confidence meter up the scale. Even just one new habit has significant positive attributes.

Habit #1: Twenty-Minute Reading Habit

Reading is a great way to stimulate your mind. Reading personal development material keeps you motivated while leveling up your skills in new techniques and strategies. If you are not working on self-improvement a little bit everyday then you risk falling into the habit of doing the same things again and again and probably getting the same results.

Reading the kind of books that make you better today than you were yesterday increases mindfulness and sharpens your overall mental health. This is a solid investment in personal growth.

If your life feels stagnant and you want to change your routine, start reading the kind of material that drives successful people to succeed at what they do best. Spend twenty minutes a day reading a book on motivation, spirituality, money investment, success principles, overcoming fear, or another topic you have a deep interest in.

Do not just sit still and accept life as it is. You can create it in whatever way you desire, but nobody is going to show you how it is done. You have to get out there and make it happen.

I have read hundreds of personal development books over the years with themes ranging from goal setting, habit development, success strategies, and time management. All of these books have had tremendous influence on my choices in life. I made better decisions, improved clarity and focus, and created a new world of opportunity because I put in the time to read the right books. There is a list of books I recommend below.

Action Step #1

Choose a personal development book that you like. You can pick one from the list I have included here [listed below].

Spend twenty minutes a day reading by blocking off that time. I like to use the **Pomodoro Technique** for time blocking. Do this early in the evening and then, if the book has any action steps such as goal setting or visualization, practice that after reading. Of course, twenty minutes is just a recommended time; you can read it for as long as you want.

Action Step #2

Share the books you read with others. Tell them what you have learned through reading and motivate them to take action. If you can, gift a good book to a friend and support each other on your journey.

Below is a list of twelve books you can start with to begin leveling up your game. Make the time to read and you will start to see positive results in both your mindset and attitude.

My twelve best recommendations to get you started:

- *The One Thing* by Gary Keller
- *Rejection Proof* by Jia Jiang
- *Awaken the Giant Within* by Tony Robbins
- *A New Earth: Awakening to Your Life's Purpose* by Eckhart Tolle
- *Essentialism: The Disciplined Pursuit of Less* by Greg McKeown
- *The Miracle Morning: The 6 Habits That Will Transform Your Life (Before 8AM)* by Hal Elrod
- *Living Forward: A Proven Plan to Stop Drifting and Get the Life You Want* by Michael Hyatt and Daniel Harkavy
- *The Art of Work: A Proven Path to Discovering What You Were Meant to Do* by Jeff Goins
- *The 7 Habits of Highly Effective People: Powerful Lessons in Personal Change* by Stephen R. Covey
- *The Power of Positive Thinking: 10 Traits for Maximum Results* by Dr. Norman Vincent Peale
- *The Success Principles* by Jack Canfield
- *Habit Stacking* by S.J. Scott

How to Speed Up Your Reading

Like most people you may struggle to find the time for most things. Reading is an activity that you cannot afford to pass by so I will give you three simple steps I used to read over forty books last year.

Read first thing in the morning. Wake up, drink a glass of water, and open a book. Bypass your email or even looking at the computer until you have put in thirty minutes of reading time.

If you are reading on a device or using the kindle app on your computer or tablet then refrain from checking email or doing anything else. You might have to get up half an hour early to get your reading time in. It is well worth it. This is a positive investment in your personal development.

Choose material that is in line with your goals. There is no point in reading something you do not like. Choose a topic that is in line with your current objectives. For example, I am starting to declutter my house. The book I am focusing on now is *Getting Things Done* by David Allen.

Take Advantage of Small Pockets of Time. Do you get agitated standing in line? How about waiting for an appointment? I am never bored when I have to wait for someone else. You can carry a Kindle reader with you. Or put the Kindle app on your phone or tablet. You have an instant library available for reading anytime.

Action Plan: Set up thirty minutes for focused reading. This can be in the morning or anytime throughout the day. I struggle with reading at night but it works for many people to read before bed. Set a timer, choose your book, and go.

Habit #2: Twenty-Minute Exercise Routine

When life gets busy exercise is one of those activities that we neglect to do. Over time your muscles start to wither away, you move less, and you place blame on yourself for being lazy. What you really need is a short, intensive exercise routine that does not take up a lot of time.

I highly recommend that you do twenty minutes of exercise each day either at home, in the office, or even when driving. This does not have to involve going to the gym; many people do not have the time [or money] for that anyways. You can do great exercises right at home in a short time without the extra cost or time. This could include stretching, yoga, push-ups, or intensity training.

Exercise is a way for you to feel great. Working out just in short bursts gives you an energy boost, and not just physically but mentally as well. You will feel refreshed and more alive.

You will discover that when you are doing something positive for yourself, it is hard to sit around and think about your problems or dwell on past events that just recreate old pains. Exercise puts you in a positive state.

When it comes to battling rejection, getting your body into shape stimulates your mind to form a more positive image of yourself. That self-rejection you struggled with will be stamped out. By not exercising you are leaving yourself prone to weight gain, stress, and increasing your chances of getting sick.

Here is a short, 10-minute exercise routine I do three times a week.

Push Ups [2x sets of 10].

You can just use your "palms flat on the floor" version or, purchase a Push-Up Bar that elevates your body while offering stability and hits your muscles harder. Try two sets of these and build up as you go.

Jump rope: It's free and can be done anywhere. I carry a rope with me for those days I am away for the day. Jumping rope increases your blood circulation and is much better than running with less impact on your joints.

You can try 1 set of 50 and then work your way up. If you can do 4 sets x 100 every morning you are giving yourself a tremendous start to the day.

Side Planks: 1 set x 20. Here is a simple version for performing the side plank.

- Start on your side with both feet together and one forearm directly below your shoulder.
- Contract your core and raise your hips until your body is in a straight line from head to feet.
- Hold the position. Don't let your hips drop for the allotted time for each set. Repeat on the other side.
- Time: You can start slow 10-second sets and work your way up.

Lunges: 1 set x 20. Here is a simple version for performing the lunge exercise:

- Keep your upper body straight, with your shoulders back and chin up. Don't look down. Pick a point directly in front of you to stare at so you don't look down. Always engage your core.
- Step forward with one leg, lowering your hips until both knees are bent at about a 90-degree angle.
- Repeat until your set is complete.

There are many variations of home exercises you can do. Are you are stuck in an office all day? You might be sitting at a desk but you can still take advantage of this.

- Calf Raises [sitting]
- Stretching
- Fist curls
- Chair Brace

Exercising for just twenty minutes a day is a major game changer. Lethargy sets in when we just succumb to our schedule or environment. We use excuses such as: "I just can't get to the gym," or "I don't have time," yet many people spend eight hours a day sitting down in an office. You do have time. You just have to tap into how to best use the time you have.

Action Plan: Schedule twenty minutes a day for exercising. If that is difficult, make it ten minutes.

Habit #3: Practice Meditation

When was the last time you actually just stopped, sat down, and did nothing? In today's world of being constantly active, the idea of doing nothing or just allowing yourself to be bored is a rarity. You are surrounded by more distractions, more entertainment, and more ways to escape from reality than ever before. And yet, being bored and doing nothing is just what you need at times.

Years ago, I learned the importance of having a fifteen minute break from the world. I would find a quiet spot where nobody could interrupt and disengage from the noise. This meant putting away the distractions and letting myself just be.

Meditating for just short spurts a day is a great habit to make you more relaxed while reducing stress levels. You will build increased concentration and focus. By letting your thoughts go and clearing your mind until you feel totally relaxed you can bring greater balance into your day.

Meditation can be difficult at first if you are not used to it. But you can do it anywhere regardless of how much noise pollution surrounds you. Meditation is nothing more than training your mind to move into a silent place that already exists. You just have to find it and then, once there, focus on staying in that place for as long as you can.

It is easy to start meditating. Here is a simple process I use that works:

- Situate yourself in a secluded location. This can be a room at home or if you are in the middle of a workday, you might have an empty room or space not being used at the office.
- Turn off devices and anything else that could distract you.
- Sit comfortably, close your eyes, and begin deep breathing.
- Observe your thoughts. You don't have to do anything about them. Just let them go.
- Stay focused on breathing. Absorb the sounds and sensations around you.
- Focus on your awareness of the environment.
- Try meditating twice a day. It has so many positive health benefits for both your mind and body.

Once you become experienced at meditating, you will be able to do it anywhere, even on a crowded train or bus. You can focus on your breathing at any time, and move your mind into that quiet space. And yes, meditation is a great practice for dealing with rejection, too!

Action Steps

Make a habit of disengaging for ten to fifteen minutes a day several times a day if possible. Just do nothing for the time you are in the zone. Get comfortable with yourself.

Turn off and tune out all distractions. You will find your mind making mental to-do lists and thinking about what needs to be done the next day. But just maintain focus on your breathing; concentrate on every breath coming in and then being exhaled. Do this for fifteen minutes and follow up with some light stretching.

If you have time you can do this twice a day. Once in the morning after waking up, and then in the evening as you start to wind down for the day. At the end of the day our mind and body start shutting down. You should mentally switch off after nine in the evening.

Put yourself into a quiet state. If you have a family or children, wait until they are asleep and then take time out for yourself instead of just wrapping up the night with TV or mindless games.

This is a great habit that will pay you back ten fold. It increases focus and sharpens your mind. You will feel alert and ready the next day. It improves sleep and increases the quality of your life in many ways.

Habit #4: Practice Journal Writing

Writing is an essential part of the recovery process. It puts your thoughts and feelings out there instead of holding everything in and letting it fester into a nasty mess. As we already looked at throughout this book, writing is one of the means of getting connected with yourself. Now what if you were to develop it into a daily or weekly habit to share your process with others? Blogging is a great way to do this.

You can easily set up a blog by signing up for hosting or using a free hosting site. I recommend signing up with a paid host server. For just a few dollars a month you can get your thoughts out there and share them with like-minded people who are going through the same things as you or have a similar interest as you do.

This could also be a great way to reach out and help someone. If social exclusion has always been a stumbling block for you, there are undoubtedly thousands out there still hiding in the shadows of their shame. You could pass along what you now know and help them to move toward recovery.

Action Steps

Go to a web server such as *Hostgator* and sign up for hosting. Have you never blogged before? That's okay! *Wordpress* has their own site with tutorials, or you can check out these great sites such as *Theblogbuilders* or *Robcubbon* where they can walk you through the steps of setting up your own site as well as providing video tutorials, blog posts, and direct support on how to set up and start blogging.

The other advantage of blogging is that it gets you to interact with other people. It is a great way to expand on your relationships by building a network of friends spanning across the globe while helping them learn something interesting and learn about you. How great is that? Since I started interacting more online I have connected with thousands of people I otherwise would not have met. This has had a positive impact on raising my self-esteem and confidence in many ways.

Habit #5: Spend Five Minutes a Day Talking to Someone (you don't know)

I used to avoid meeting new people because my core pain point was in danger of being judged. I thought that if I started to have a conversation with someone, it would not take long before he or she had me figured out. Or I would usually say something stupid, or say nothing at all, being unable to add to the conversation. So I avoided contact and kept every interaction brief with emotions off the table. This isn't a good strategy for making friends.

But reaching out to people we do not know is a sure-fire way to recover from the fear of rejection. It eliminates your rejection avoidance issues if you have any. What I discovered is that many people feel the same way. They are walking around being afraid to engage with anyone, so they keep to themselves. People want to communicate and share with the world. By being the first to open up and say: "How are you doing today?" you could be adding great value to someone's day.

Now, this habit is hard to implement at first. You may still be feeling like "that's just not me," or "what if they just ignore me or think I'm weird?" I can tell you that when I started to put myself out there and I did not care what people thought, my spontaneity exploded. I was meeting people all the time. And those memories stick. Just start with small steps.

Who do I reach out to?

Talk to someone in your company with whom you have never spoken with before or just in brief encounters. Even if it is just a "Good morning!" that is something. By opening up you start to heal quickly and, the other person feels important as well. If they do not reciprocate or are just feeling unfriendly, then so be it. It is not your problem. Go to someone else.

Action Steps

This week, engage in a conversation with someone you do not know. You do not have to walk up to complete strangers. Do it when you go shopping. Have a conversation with the salesperson or cashier. The reason this is important is that it gets you out of the comfort zone.

If the feelings of inferiority have been with you for most of your life, nothing works better than just putting yourself out there. Just say, "To hell with the fear!" and approach people. You would be amazed how people respond to you when you treat them as if they mattered.

If you need help with social confidence and the courage to talk to people in social situations, you can check out *The Art of Witty Banter* by **Patrick King** for additional support.

Habit #6: Make a List of Goals That Inspire You

Writing out your goals is a great habit to move yourself towards taking positive action. You can create a goal portfolio in just a matter of a few hours. With your goals set, you will achieve things that you have always dreamt of but never seemed possible.

I recommend this simple process for setting your goals:

Write down something you have always wanted to do or achieve. Do you want to take a trip? Write a book? Save more money for retirement? I want you to dream big and start writing down all the things you have ever wanted to do and achieve, especially those things that you have always been ashamed to tell anyone!

For years I wrote books and articles, but because of my shame-based personality I never told anyone! I was publishing books on Amazon and keeping quiet about it. That is crazy, but that is what happens when you struggle with the fear of rejection. Even your greatest achievements go unrecognized because you are afraid that somebody is going to find out about it. Let's change that today.

Whatever it is, write down just one goal for now and then use the following process for taking action towards all of your goals.

Take a look at one of your goals and write down five action steps you could take to get moving on it. Is there a course you have to sign up for? A book you have to read? Someone you have to call? Gather some important info from the Internet? Whatever it is, all that matters is that you do something. TAKE ACTION!

Set a completion date. Deciding on a deadline is a very important action. Without a deadline, you could work on your goal forever. Some goals take years to complete; others can be done in a week or less. Regardless, give a concrete date to finish your goal.

Be accountable to others. Years ago when I started working on my goals, the one area I always failed at was following through on a deadline. And the reason for this was because I had nobody to hold me accountable.

Once you have set your completion date [writing a book, setting your travel plans] let someone know about it. Hell, let everyone know about it. Join an accountability group or put it out there on your Twitter or Facebook. Let everyone know what you are doing. This will create a sense of urgency, which you will find particularly motivating. You can also make a deal with an accountability partner.

If you cannot achieve your goal by a certain date, you will give them [fill in amount here] dollars. Holding yourself accountable is a great way to getting things done. It is the main reason I was able to finish this book on time!

Action Steps

1. Block off three hours during this week to write down your goals. Be clear on what you want. Do this for the next three days.

2. Block off one hour for the next three days [or thirty minutes if time is tight] to develop your goal portfolio.

3. Make it a habit to review your goals at the end of the week.

4. Decide on the specific mini-tasks you will do to move you closer towards achieving your goals.

Habit #7: Plan Your Daily MITs

I made this a habit several months ago and I have not looked back. What you do is this: Before you go to bed OR first thing in the morning, write down the three most important tasks that you are going to do that day.

How it basically works is that, you write down your three most important tasks for the day. Then choose the first task that is the most important of the three and get to work on it. Are you writing a blog? Exercising? This goes hand in hand with the habits featured here and gets you focused on new and fun activities.

How to set your MITs:

1. Write down your three MITs for this day. Your MITs ideally should be related to your current goals for maximum effectiveness.
2. Do your MITs first thing in the morning. If you cannot do everything in the morning due to time constraints, choose the one that you can do. Then, throughout the day, schedule time for tackling the remaining tasks.

If you cannot finish everything today, move the unfinished tasks to the next day. Then, pick up where you left off the next morning. Keep tackling your list and do what is difficult first.

Action Steps

To do these I created the habit of waking up early. By getting up at an earlier time I was able to focus more intensely on what I needed to get done based on my goals for that day/week. If you are struggling with time, you may have to adjust your schedule by going to bed earlier or cutting out on distractions that are wasting time.

Habit #8: Develop the Learning Habit

Is there a new skill you want to learn? A course that you have been thinking about taking to expand your business? A hobby that you want to excel at? Then if so, the learning habit is the way to get started.

In an age of information where we have access to anything it is hard to know where to begin. It feels like we are learning all the time with the amount of information coming in on a regular basis. This is why I suggest that you create a learning habit by committing to a time of day that you can focus and concentrate on the subject you want to learn. If not, you will likely end up chasing everything.

By committing to learning something new, you are increasing your chances of getting a better job, making more money, or advancing in your personal development. Take all three of these advantages and building a dedicated learning session into your routine becomes a no-brainer.

You can learn anything you want to if you know what it is you want to learn. The key is to decide what it is you want to learn. This is also the challenge as we are being tempted by so many other books, courses and information scrambling for our attention.

Here is a **simple 7-step plan**:

1. Identify the skill you want to learn. Write this down.

2. Decide how you will learn this skill. Is it an online course through **Teachable** or **udemi**? Will you go to a school or hire a teacher/mentor/coach? Decide the way you will do your training.

3. Connect with the people who you can learn from. Do you have other people around you interested in the same thing? Building a tribe around your area of interest is critical to learning because they can provide you with support when you need it.

4. Decide when you will learn. I find that having a fixed schedule works best when committing to learning a new skill. Doing it when you feel like it means that you'll slack off when the training gets difficult.

5. Decide how much is enough. Are you looking to master this skill, or do you just need to get to a certain level of proficiency?

6. Decide why this is important. What are you looking to gain?

7. Choose your course of action. What actions can you take right now to start moving towards this? What actions do you need to take consistently to learn this skill? For example, if I am learning guitar, I may have to sign up for lessons and practice regularly twice a week.

Action Steps

Decide the skill you want to master and why. Set up a plan to learn and join up with a group of supporter who can hold you accountable. Learn as much as you can and then when you are satisfied, you can put your new skill to work. Or you might decide to move onto another learning curve.

Habit #9: Focus on Being in the Present Moment

Spiritual teacher **Eckhart Tolle**, the bestselling author of *The Power of Now*, wrote, "If your mind carries a heavy burden of past, you will experience more of the same. The past perpetuates itself through lack of presence. The quality of your consciousness at this moment is what shapes the future."

The emotions you have of feeling powerless, inadequate, and inferior are all connected to the past. This keeps the cycle going. When I read this book years ago, it put everything into a new perspective for me. I would like to share this with you.

When you live in the past, that is, when your emotions and thoughts continually run through a cycle that keeps the past events active, you tap into those pain points again and again. It is like putting your finger in an electrical outlet and knowing that you are going to get zapped. But because it is your nature to do what is familiar, people who live in a shame-based lifestyle revert back to this day after day.

This can all change right now.

I already shared with you a technique that you can use to stop this cycle from repeating itself. Make it a habit to focus on your NOW. This will become one of the most important habits you implement. It was for me, but in order for it to happen you have to stay present, and staying present means observing what is happening right now and not what has happened in the past.

It is amazing the power that the past can have on our lives decades later. People who work on their recovery are often surprised when they suddenly realize how they were feeding into that power day after day for years.

The present has power too. You can focus on that power right now. And to that end, make it a habit to stay present. When you find yourself drifting back into memories of the past that trigger your state of inadequacy, bring yourself back.

Create a trigger symbol that keeps you present. A friend of mine wore a colored band around his wrist. When he looked at it, he remembered to stay present. Set your smartphone to chime every so often as a trigger.

Within a few months, you will find that instead of spending seventy percent of your thoughts lost in negative feelings by reliving experiences that ended long ago, you can now enjoy seventy percent more of your life by staying present. Then all you have to look forward to is what is happening now. It is one of the best ways to energize your life. Stay present. Stay in the NOW.

Habit #10: The Money Saving Habit

Money is important. While it may not be everything, having money is certainly better than not having it or being in debt and owing more than you have. While saving money is challenging, it does not have to be difficult. If you make it a habit, you can start saving today regardless of your current financial situation.

Here are a few suggestions for saving money:

Reduce Your Expenses. We all have bills to pay. But some of these bills are unnecessary and could be costing you hundreds [or thousands] of dollars per year. Make a list of the monthly expenses you pay out and ask yourself if there is anything on the list you could either: reduce in the amount of money spent, or eliminate completely.

For example, I recently canceled my newspaper subscription. It was costing $32.00 a month and nobody was reading it. Take a look at things such as: subscriptions or memberships that you might be paying for but no longer using.

Another expense that was costing hundreds per month was eating out at restaurants. By making your lunch at home and taking it to work, you could save a couple hundred dollars a month.

Shop around before buying. When you need something, it pays to compare. Before buying on impulse, look around at various places before making a purchase. Amazon tends to have the lowest prices but there are times I could find cheaper items at a discount shop. It doesn't always have to be new and shiny. Buying used stuff instead of always going for new can save you thousands in $$$.

Borrow items instead of buying. I do buy quite a few books, mostly on impulse through Amazon or at the local bookstore. But you can borrow most books for free. And, if the library doesn't have it, check because they may be able to order it if they have a budget for buying new books.

Pay yourself first. Set up an automatic withdrawal system so that, for every paycheck, you have 10% taken right away. Check your financial situation first to make sure this won't leave you short if money is tight. If 10% isn't doable, you can start with 5%. Put it this way: even if you only put away $100 a month, that is better than nothing, which is what many people end up saving.

In fact, the majority of people are borrowing cash to make ends meet to keep up with mounting bills and expenses. Once you have this worked out, set it up and let it run automatically. $100 doesn't sound like much money, but if you did it for ten years, you'd have over 10G saved. That's' a great start for a future nest egg.

Decide a set amount of money you will save each week or month [depending on how often you get paid]. Decide why you need this money and what it is for. Then set up a system so that you are making your savings plan automatic. This is a great way to save and is the preferred recommended strategy of **David Bach**, the author of *The Automatic Millionaire*.

Habit #11: Assimilate Positive Affirmations

This habit is great for building positive energy, and if you have been suffering from feelings of inadequacy and inferiority most of your life, there is nothing wrong with having more positivity. In fact, it is the only medicine you need. Affirmations and quotes are a great way to rewire your thoughts.

Years ago, when I started to recover from several self-defeating behaviors, a mentor of mine gave me great advice on how to be more positive. He said "Read three quotes a day: one in the morning, one at lunch, and one after dinner. Then, before bed, read all three again."

Within a few weeks, I was walking around reciting these quotes, and they were powerful words that replaced my negative vocabulary. Throughout this book, I used some of these quotes, but I would like to share with you below a short list of ten quotes you can start with right now.

These quotes are from my personal list of favorites that reframed my thinking and I still read on a daily basis.

1. "If fear is cultivated it will become stronger, if faith is cultivated it will achieve mastery." — **John Paul Jones**
2. "You gain strength, courage, and confidence by every experience in which you really stop to look fear in the face. You are able to say to yourself, 'I lived through this horror. I can take the next thing that comes along.'" — **Eleanor Roosevelt**
3. "When I started counting my blessings, my whole life turned around." — **Willie Nelson**
4. "Always be yourself, express yourself, have faith in yourself, do not go out and look for a successful personality and duplicate it." — **Bruce Lee**
5. "We all learn lessons in life. Some stick, some don't. I have always learned more from rejection and failure than from acceptance and success." — **Henry Rollins**
6. "It takes a little bit of mindfulness and a little bit of attention to others to be a good listener, which helps cultivate emotional nurturing and engagement." — **Deepak Chopra**
7. "Your net worth to the world is usually determined by what remains after your bad habits are subtracted from your good ones." — **Benjamin Franklyn**
8. "Doing what you love is the cornerstone of having abundance in your life." — **Wayne Dyer**
9. "Two roads diverged in a wood and I - I took the one less traveled by, and that has made all the difference." — **Robert Frost**
10. "Life is a gift, and it offers us the privilege, opportunity, and responsibility to give something back by becoming more." — **Tony Robbins**

Action Steps

Make it a morning habit of reading a list of your favorite quotes. This is a positive action that will set your thoughts for the day. Write the quotes down in a notebook and keep them close by, or mark them on your PC or tablet.

Recite them during the day when you feel anxiety or experiencing a stressful situation. One suggestion is to add to your list of quotes by one a day. At the end of one year you'll have 365 great quotes of wisdom.

Habit #12: Practice the Gratitude Habit

I use to avoid giving out compliments at all costs unless there was something in it for me. Again, giving a compliment meant leaving myself vulnerable. So I would not do it unless I had to. But compliments are another great way to forge amazing relationships. Who does not like to be complimented on a job well done or to be told they look nice?

Some people might rebuff it because they are not used to it. Like you, maybe they have low esteem and rejectionist issues (remember that you are not alone). So give a compliment once a day for a week. Then start to do it twice a day for a second week.

After that, make a game out of it and keep track of how many compliments you give. There is nothing like strong encouragement to make someone feel good, and it is another strong step toward your self-improvement.

Here are a few compliments you can start with:

- Tell your partner or kids how amazing they are.
- Tell someone what a great job they did on something.
- Tell your partner or spouse how nice he or she looks today.

Compliments are difficult at first because as practicing rejectionists we are always looking for reassurance from someone else. The problem with this is that it feeds into our need for feeling like we have to get permission from others before we can feel good about ourselves. This results in a very self-centered approach, and when you wait around for someone to tell you how great you are it becomes an expectation.

So reverse the action. Give it away, and what you give away you will receive back twice as much. But do not give with the expectation of receiving something in return. Accept it as a gift when and if you do.

Creating New Routines

By building a new routine you change the way you behave. When you change your behavior you shift your mindset, priorities, and the way you think. A new routine takes work, and you will feel some resistance at first. That is why you should only focus on building one small routine at a time.

For example: I wake up early, drink a glass of water, do twenty minutes of quick exercises, drink another glass of water, and then read for twenty minutes. It is a simple routine, but I am doing something for my health (exercise and hydration), personal growth (reading), and peace of mind.

Now you have choices that will define you. Not just any choice, but life empowering choices that only you can make. As you finish reading this book I hope you think about some of those choices you would like to make.

Working on Small Habits

Take a brief look at the habits again and think "small stuff." Focus on the little things you can do to avoid getting overwhelmed. It takes time to implement those strategies as habits.

If you want to make big changes, you can do this by focusing on small steps done with purpose. For example, remember that if you want to help someone, you do not have to help everyone at once. Just focus on doing one good thing for one person. Then repeat this again the next day.

If you want to work on replacing a negative belief, focus on one or two positive affirmations that target that belief. Do this for ten to fourteen days. You WILL see big results in time. Then move onto the next negative belief.

Refer to the negative beliefs we talked about in chapter two or target a specific belief you have. There is a solution for everything, and by focusing on the little stuff you can avoid getting overwhelmed by thinking that you have to do it all.

But if you focus and work on it a little one day at a time, you will gain your confidence, reduce stress and worry, and feel great about who you are and how far you have come. This is not just motivational fluff but real facts. Do what matters a little bit every day, and make it your priority.

Anthony Robbins said:

> *"We often overestimate what we can achieve in a year and significantly underestimate all we can achieve in a decade."*

Think of your life as a long-term project. You are planning it every day in small increments. Set aside one hour a day for the next 30 days to develop your life plan.

What you can achieve in one hour will amaze you if you stay committed to carving out the life you have always wanted to lead.

Conclusion

Preparing for Your Journey

"The journey was a surreal dream. This world was about knowing the person you'd always wanted to be and setting your foot down to it, remembering the person you'd thought you were as a child and rejoicing in its living, breathing actuality."

— **Christopher Hawke**

This book, *Rejection Reset*, is a book of action, faith, and perseverance. It was written with a single purpose in mind:

To give you the courage, hope, strength, skills, and personal power to live your life free of rejection.

Now that you have read this book, what do you think? Are you ready to take your life to the next level? Can you break beyond the criticism, gripes, and old mindset of yesterday?

I know you can. Your rejection free journey is just beginning.

You can do anything if you stay focused on what you truly want. When you no longer fear rejection but embrace it as a necessary challenge, you will discover that this journey is a wonderful opportunity to embrace your dreams and rise up to a new level of greatness.

The world is not always a welcoming place, but that is because it is full of fearful people. They are looking for a way out of that fear. They need someone to show them what it is like to confront the fears that are stopping them from taking action and living their dreams.

Now that you have some solid skills to work with and you know that you are the creator of your own success, you can show others how to confront the rejection pushing them back and keeping them scared. By doing it scared, we can train our fear to do anything.

Now, let's wrap it up with **four key lessons** to take home.

(1). **Imagine the reality that is yours.** Just take a moment to get yourself into a relaxed frame of mind. Find a quiet spot and clear your head of all thoughts. Now bring yourself into this present moment.

Ask yourself this question: "What could I do with my life if rejection is no longer keeping me scared? What dreams could I accomplish? What relationships could I create? What actions would I take?"

Imagine what can be yours and you can have it.

Reset your day with a renewed vision and expand on your ideas for creating a better life for yourself. Do things differently than you did the day before. Make friends and deepen your relationships with people who are walking a similar journey. In time you will be rewarded with a renewed sense of confidence and a powerful mindset fashioned out of courage and a willingness to never give up.

(2). **Healing is a journey.** It is a lifelong journey. Give yourself time to absorb the lessons of life. Continue to seek the answers to questions and always be asking more.

Small changes day by day and actions practiced consistently over time, while keeping your mind focused on the moment, will produce results that work. You may not see any changes right away, but if you work on expanding yourself just a little every day, within a few months, check out how you are feeling. You should notice a considerable difference in your confidence and approach toward people.

(3). **Rejection is a point of view.** If someone rejects you for something [your idea is not good enough, you are not their type, or you are not the kind of person "we" are looking for] remember that not everyone can have everything.

People with the best looks and amazing talents are still rejected. But when we get turned down, we turn it into a personal vendetta. We might even contemplate a way to get back at that person. You might start to have a line of negative thinking that says, "I'll show him a thing or two!"

For whatever reasons you got a NO, there are also many people out there who have said YES. Looking back on your life, you've probably had more "YES" than "NO." Have you ever succeeded at getting a job? Making a new friend? Getting someone to go out on a date with you? Then most of your life has been made up of acceptance and only a small percentage is rejection.

The odds are in your favor. If you get a YES, you win. If you get a NO, you still win, because the rejection makes you stronger.

(4). **Continue to reject rejection.** When you are no longer afraid of being rejected, you are deciding to empower your life when rejection happens. Amazing opportunities appears when you change your perspective; that is to say, when you start to see rejection as something that can help you and not just hurt you.

The things that do not defeat you give you thicker skin. Why should rejection be any different? Why let it win?

Throughout this book we looked at many strategies for gaining confidence in social situations, like developing your personal power and becoming less scared of the disastrous outcome you were convinced was real. But now we know: The power of rejection exists inside of you. It is yours to own. This means, you can disown it by choosing to reject it.

Do you want to reset the way you have been living? Do you want to stop being a victim of rejection?

Then do not play by its rules. You can reject rejection and be yourself in social parties, on a date, or at home with your family.

The healing starts as soon as you choose to say NO. You can refuse to listen to the negative voices in your mind telling you, "There, you see, rejected again." You can choose to be more outgoing, more confident, and more proactive. You can choose your thoughts and ideas.

Too often we wait for things to change. We wait too long. So stop waiting and start taking action. What is holding you back right now? Is it the idea or belief that you could get rejected, and that would shatter your universe?

If you are doing nothing to change the way you are living your life, you will attract more of the fear holding you where you are. The ability to face rejection again and again builds mental toughness.

Define Your Success

I encourage you to continue to refer to this book whenever you feel like a rejection has defeated you. Refer to it whenever you need a refresher.

Success is best defined when two people work together to overcome impossible challenges. You are not alone in this. We all need to raise each other up so that we can stand on the shoulders of giants and be the best that we can be.

Ask yourself what success means to you. What do you want to accomplish in your lifetime? Who do you want to help along the way? What are you willing to accept, and what will you reject? Keep asking questions to yourself. You will find the answers in time. Continue being a seeker on the journey towards living a better life.

Remember: *You can reset your life, your day, or this minute. You can start over or you can start from where you have never begun before.*

Just keep pushing forward and never give up. You have got this. Do not look back, unless you plan on going that way.

All the best,

Scott Allan

"The cave you fear to enter holds the treasure you seek."

— **Joseph Campbell,** author of
The Man With a Thousand Faces

About Scott Allan

Scott Allan is a bestselling author who has a passion for teaching, building life skills, and inspiring others to take charge of their lives.

Scott's mission is to give people the strategies needed to design the life they want through choice.

He believes successful living is a series of small, consistent actions taken every day to build a thriving lifestyle with intentional purpose.

By taking the necessary steps and eliminating unwanted distractions that keep you stuck, you are free to focus on the essentials.

You can connect with Scott online at:

Blog: www.scottallanauthor.com

Amazon Books: amazon.com/author/scottallan

What Did You Think of *Rejection Reset?*

First of all, thank you for purchasing this book *Rejection Reset*. I know you could have picked any number of books to read, but you picked this book and for that I am extremely grateful.

If you enjoyed this book and found some benefit in reading this, I'd like to hear from you and hope that you could take some time to **post a review on Amazon**.

Your feedback and support will help this author to greatly improve his writing craft for future projects and make this book even better.

All the best,

Scott Allan

https://scottallanauthor.com

Read the Next Book in the Rejection Free Series

Visit amazon.com/author/scottallan to buy **Rejection Free** Today.

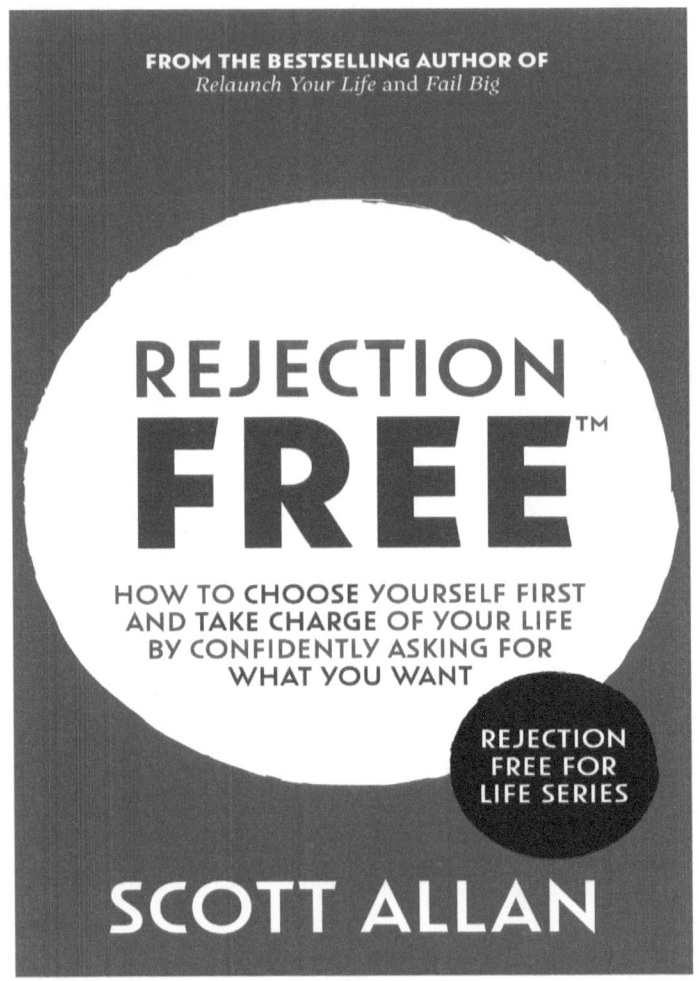

Books by Scott Allan

Check out these other bestselling books by Scott Allan. You can visit his website at www.scottallaninternational.com to stay up to date on all future book releases, or amazon.com/author/scottallan

Empower Your Thoughts: Control Worry and Anxiety, Develop a Positive Mental Attitude, and Master Your Mindset

Empower Your Fear: Leverage Your Fears To Rise Above Mediocrity and Turn Self-Doubt Into a Confident Plan of Action

Empower Your Success: Success Strategies to Maximize Performance, Take Positive Action, and Engage Your Enthusiasm for Living a Great Life

Rejection Reset: A Strategic Step-By-Step Program for Restoring Self-Confidence, Reshaping an Inferior Mindset, and Thriving In a Shame-Free Lifestyle

Rejection Free: How To Choose Yourself First and Take Charge of Your Life By Confidently Asking For What You Want

Do It Scared: Charge Forward With Confidence, Conquer Resistance, and Break Through Your Limitations

Relaunch Your Life: Break the Cycle of Self-Defeat, Destroy Negative Emotions, and Reclaim Your Personal Power

Drive Your Destiny: Create a Vision for Your Life, Build Better Habits for Wealth and Health, and Unlock Your Inner Greatness

The Discipline of Masters: Destroy Big Obstacles, Master Your Time, Capture Creative Ideas and Become the Leader You Were Born to Be

The Master of Achievement: Conquer Fear and Adversity, Maximize Big Goals, Supercharge Your Success and Develop a Purpose Driven Mindset

Undefeated: Persevere in the Face of Adversity, Master the Art of Never Giving Up, and Always Beat the Odds Stacked Against You

Fail Big, Expanded Edition: Fail Your Way to Success and Break All the Rules to Get There

www.ingramcontent.com/pod-product-compliance
Lightning Source LLC
Chambersburg PA
CBHW021446070526
44577CB00002B/273